IN THE SIERRA
MOUNTAIN WRITINGS
BY KENNETH REXROTH

ALSO BY KENNETH REXROTH

Available from New Directions

An Autobiographical Novel

Classics Revisited

Collected Longer Poems

Collected Shorter Poems

More Classics Revisited

100 Poems from the Chinese

100 More Poems from the Chinese:
  Love and the Turning Year

100 Poems from the Japanese

100 More Poems from the Japanese

Selected Poems

Songs of Love, Moon & Wind

Women Poets of China

Women Poets of Japan

World Outside the Window: Selected Essays

KENNETH REXROTH IN THE SIERRA

IN THE SIERRA
MOUNTAIN WRITINGS
BY KENNETH REXROTH

EDITED BY
KIM STANLEY ROBINSON

A NEW DIRECTIONS BOOK

Design by Sylvia Frezzolini Severance
Manufactured in the United States of America
First published as a New Directions Paperbook (NDP1228) in 2012.
New Directions Books are printed on acid-free paper.

The editor, Kim Stanley Robinson, wishes to thank Bradford Morrow, Gary Snyder, Sean O'Grady, Carter Scholz, Terry Bisson, Tom Killion, Declan Spring, Rachelle Lerner, David Robertson, and Dana Gioia. Special thanks to Ken Knabb.

Library of Congress Cataloging-in-Publication Data
Rexroth, Kenneth, 1905–1982.
In the Sierra : mountain writings / by Kenneth Rexroth ; edited by Kim Stanley Robinson.
p. cm.
ISBN 978-0-8112-1902-0 (acid-free paper) —   ISBN 978-0-8112-1989-1
1. Rexroth, Kenneth, 1905–1982. 2. Sierra Nevada (Calif. and Nev.)—Literary collections.
I. Robinson, Kim Stanley. II. Title.
PS3535.E923I5 2012
818'.52—dc23

                                    2012002757

10 9 8 7 6 5 4 3

New Directions Books are published for James Laughlin
by New Directions Publishing Corporation
80 Eighth Avenue, New York 10011
ndbooks.com

Introduction *xv*
Map *xx*

Kenneth Rexroth's Mountain Poetry

From IN WHAT HOUR (1940)

Climbing Milestone Mountain, August 22, 1937 *3*
North Palisade, the End of September, 1939 *5*
Hiking on the Coast Range *6*
On What Planet *7*
Toward an Organic Philosophy *8*
Falling Leaves and Early Snow *12*
The Heart Unbroken and the Courage Free *13*
Value In Mountains *13*
A Lesson in Geography *17*
Ice Shall Cover Nineveh *21*

From THE ART OF WORLDLY WISDOM (1949)

In the Memory of Andrée Rexroth, part c *31*

From THE PHOENIX AND THE TORTOISE (1944)

Another Spring *32*
Night Below Zero *32*
Inversely, as the Square of Their Distances Apart *33*
Andrée Rexroth *35*
Andrée Rexroth *36*

Strength Through Joy   *37*

Incarnation   *38*

From THE SIGNATURE OF ALL THINGS (1949)

Lyell's Hypothesis Again   *40*

Blues   *42*

Andrée Rexroth   *43*

From BEYOND THE MOUNTAINS (1951)

From Hermaios   *47*

From Berenike   *48*

From THE DRAGON AND THE UNICORN (1952)

Time Spirals   *52*

Mirror   *53*

Final passage of The Dragon and the Unicorn   *54*

From IN DEFENSE OF THE EARTH (1956)

A Living Pearl   *64*

The Lights in the Sky Are Stars   *67*

Time Is the Mercy of Eternity   *75*

Mary and the Seasons   *81*

From NATURAL NUMBERS (1964)

Homer in Basic   *89*

Fish Peddler and Cobbler   *91*

From Air and Angels, Maroon Bells   *93*

From ONE HUNDRED POEMS
FROM THE CHINESE (1956)

Tu Fu / Winter Dawn   *95*
Tu Fu / A Restless Night In Camp   *95*
Tu Fu / South Wind   *96*

From ONE HUNDRED MORE POEMS
FROM THE CHINESE (1970)

Ch'u Ch'uang I / A Mountain Spring   *97*
Wang Wei / Autumn Twilight In the Mountains   *97*
Liu Ch'ang Ch'ing / Snow On Lotus Mountain   *98*
Han Yu / Amongst the Cliffs   *98*
Li Shang Yin / When Will I Be Home?   *99*
Wen T'ing Yen / In the Mountains as
   Autumn Begins   *100*

From GÖDEL'S PROOF (1965)

Yin and Yang   *101*

From THE HEART'S GARDEN,
THE GARDEN'S HEART (1967)

A Song at the Winepresses   *102*

From LOVE IS AN ART OF TIME (1974)

Your Birthday in the California Mountains   *105*
Hapax   *106*

Kenneth Rexroth's Sierra Prose

From AN AUTOBIOGRAPHICAL NOVEL
  (1964, expanded 1991)

> *From* Chapter 30   *111*
> *From* Chapter 39   *115*
> *From* Chapter 51   *119*
> *From* Chapter 52   *120*
> *From* Chapter 53   *123*
> *From* Chapter 60   *124*
> *From* Chapter 61   *125*

From CAMPING IN THE WESTERN MOUNTAINS
  (written 1939, published online 2002)

> *From* Chapter One, "Minimum Equipment"   *126*
> *From* Chapter Four, "The Camp"   *130*
> *From* Chapter Six, "Horses, Mules, Burros, Riding,
>   Packing, and Horse Furniture"   *137*
> *From* Chapter Nine, "The Trail"   *140*
> *From* Chapter Ten, "Climbing"   *142*
> *From* Chapter Twelve, "Winter Camping"   *143*

From THE WPA GUIDE TO CALIFORNIA
  (1939)

> *From* "Sequoia and General Grant National Parks"   *145*
> *From* "Yosemite National Park"   *146*

From REXROTH'S NEWSPAPER COLUMNS
in the *San Francisco Examiner*

August 7, 1960   *147*
August 14, 1960   *148*
July 2, 1961   *149*
July 12, 1961   *151*
July 8, 1962   *153*
July 11, 1962   *155*
August 26, 1962   *156*
June 30, 1963   *158*
August 18, 1963   *161*
August 21, 1963   *163*
August 23, 1964   *164*
December 2, 1964   *166*
September 13, 1965   *167*
January 24, 1966   *168*
September 11, 1966   *169*

From REXROTH'S NEWSPAPER COLUMNS
in the *San Francisco Bay Guardian*

December 1969   *171*
May 1969   *172*

Correspondence and Commentary

From KENNETH REXROTH AND JAMES LAUGHLIN:
SELECTED LETTERS (1937–1981)

Laughlin to Rexroth, June 15, 1937   *177*
Rexroth to Laughlin, October 21, 1939   *177*
Rexroth to Laughlin, May 5, 1941   *177*
Laughlin to Rexroth, May 16, 1945   *178*
Rexroth to Laughlin, April 13, 1948   *178*
Rexroth to Laughlin, June 25, 1948   *178*
Laughlin to Rexroth, December 17, 1981   *178*

From THE WAY IT WASN'T, by James Laughlin
(2006)   *180*

From BYWAYS, by James Laughlin (2005)   *182*

KENNETH REXROTH, OBSERVER, by Carter
Scholz   (2012)   *185*

NOTES   *195*

IN THE SIERRA
MOUNTAIN WRITINGS
BY KENNETH REXROTH

INTRODUCTION

KENNETH REXROTH (1905–1982) grew up in the Chicago
area, raised mostly by his mother Delia. She died when he was
twelve, and his father, who was never much involved, died when
he was fifteen. After that he lived a bohemian youth in the Roaring
Twenties, spending his teenage years as a truant anarchist and café in-
tellectual, with summer stints as a horse packer in the Pacific North-
west. At age twenty-two, he and his young wife Andrée hitchhiked
around the American West, and when they arrived in San Francisco
they settled there. "The ocean was at the end of the streetcar line.
Down the peninsula and across the Golden Gate, the Coast Range
was still a wilderness, and the High Sierras were a short day's trip
away.... We decided to stay and grow up with the town."*

For the next four decades Rexroth did that, becoming one
of San Francisco's leading intellectuals. His life was turbulent; he
married four times, raised two daughters, and made his living by
literature, though he was also at various times an organizer for the
National Maritime Union, a conscientious objector working as a
psychiatric hospital nurse, a salon host, night-school teacher, radio
personality, and newspaper columnist. Exceptionally well-read,
sure of judgment, and clear in expression, he made his journalism
into a kind of ongoing education in the humanities. He consistently
defended classicism and modernism, also Asian cultures, environ-
mental causes, and the erotic and mystical literary traditions; he
just as consistently attacked the military-industrial complex, impe-
rialism, and the New York literary establishment. He was always

---

* Kenneth Rexroth, *An Autobiographical Novel* (New Directions, 1991, p. 367).

slightly ahead of the zeitgeist, and many aspects of what we think of as California culture were early interests of his. All his activities together made him the single public intellectual most responsible for the character of the San Francisco Renaissance, which is often associated with the Beat Generation and then the Sixties.

In this tumultuous San Francisco life Rexroth always had an enduring island of calm, located on the other side of the state: the Sierra Nevada of California. This high-mountain range serves as the spine of the California landscape, extending along the east side of the state from north of Lake Tahoe to the southern end of the Great Central valley. Public land from the start, the range has become more and more protected as wilderness over the decades. Like many Californians before him and since, Rexroth took a youthful trip into the High Sierra and fell in love with the place, and for the rest of his life went back as often he could. In almost every summer from 1927 to 1967 he hiked and climbed throughout the southern Sierra, usually taking along rented horses or burros, which allowed him to stay out for a month or six weeks at a time. He also made shorter spring and fall trips, and ski toured and snow-camped in the winter. In the thirties he took a few climbing classes with the Sierra Club; these were also the years he began climbing and skiing in the Sierra with his longtime publisher and friend, James Laughlin of New Directions. In 1937 he stayed in Yosemite so long that his wife Marie had to explain to investigators from the relief rolls where he had gone. During the Second World War, gas rationing slowed him down, as it did everyone, but afterward he went to the Sierra more than ever, often renting a cabin at Grant Grove for the month of June, writing there while the snowpack was still heavy, then in August hiking or riding into the high country. He had a few hiking friends, especially Frank Triest, and he also went frequently with his wives, Andrée, Marie, and Marthe, and with his daughters Mary and Katherine in their childhood. If you were

to add all of Rexroth's time in the Sierra together it would come
to a total of around five or six years, in other words about the same
amount of time John Muir spent there.

This intense and sustained Sierra experience was crucial to
Rexroth, as he often said himself. "I have always felt I was most
myself in the mountains. There I have done the bulk of what is
called my creative work. At least it is in the mountains that I write
most of my poetry....There whatever past emotion and experi-
ence I choose to recollect and write down, take on most depth and
meaning."* Though no single book of Rexroth's was devoted to the
Sierra alone, he wrote about it often enough over the years that a
book's worth of pages accumulated. This is that book; it contains
most of what Rexroth wrote about the Sierra Nevada.

The material comes from many sources, and was written and
published over a period of about forty years, between 1937 and
1980. His mountain poems form the bulk of the book. Most of
these are set in the Sierra Nevada, but there are also some about
Mount Tamalpais in Marin County just north of San Francisco,
where Rexroth used a small sheepherder's cabin as a getaway; there
are one or two about the Rocky Mountains, and one or two about
the stars. The mountain poems among his famous translations of
classic Chinese poetry are also included. Together they make one of
the most striking and attractive groups in his overall body of work.

The second part of this book contains most of Rexroth's
prose writing about the Sierra. Like the poems, these pieces made
their first appearance in various places through the years, including
Rexroth's autobiographical novel, his newspaper columns, and a
camping handbook he wrote for the WPA, never published but
now online. A third section includes James Laughlin's few descrip-
tions of his mountain adventures with Rexroth, letters between

---

* *San Francisco Examiner*, August 7, 1960.

Rexroth and Laughlin discussing their mountain trips, and an essay by California writer Carter Scholz discussing the star references in Rexroth's poetry. These prose selections form an entertaining composite description of a style of Sierra life common to many Californians in the mid-twentieth century; they also give us some personal context for the poems, creating a kind of portrait of the artist as mountaineer.

It has been a real pleasure to gather all of Rexroth's mountain writing and realize it makes one of the great books about the Sierra Nevada. It can be thought of, perhaps, as the replacement for Rexroth's lost WPA handbook, but hugely better—something to take a permanent place on the shelf of American literature, somewhere between Muir and Snyder.

                                    KIM STANLEY ROBINSON

xx

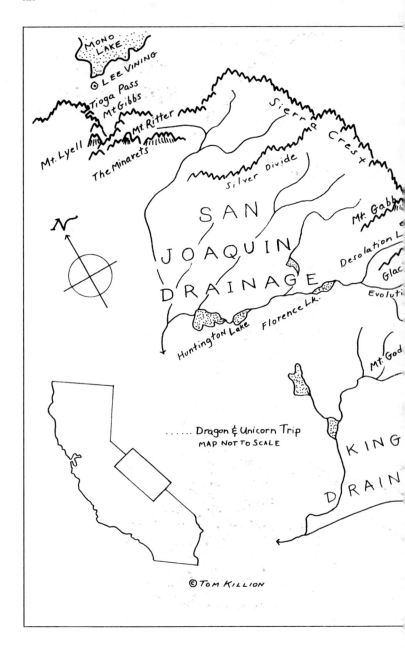

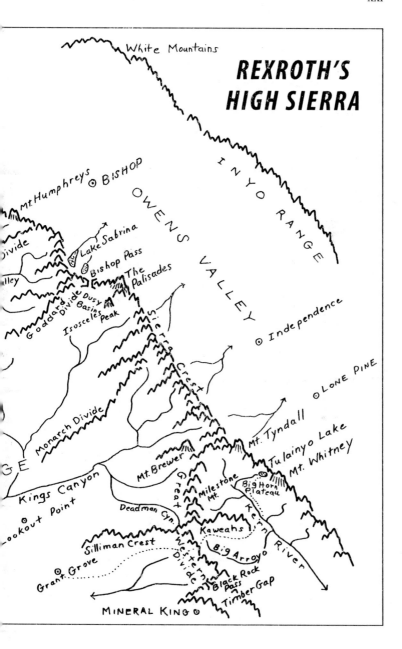

White Mountains

REXROTH'S HIGH SIERRA

INYO RANGE

Mt. Humphreys · BISHOP

OWENS VALLEY

Divide

Lake Sabrina

Bishop Pass

alley

The Palisades

Goddard Divide Dusy Basins

Isosceles Peak

Sierra Crest

Independence

LONE PINE

Monarch Divide

Mt. Tyndall

Tulainyo Lake

Mt. Whitney

GE

Mt. Brewer

Great

Milestone Mt.

Big Horn Plateau

Kings Canyon

Lookout Point

Deadman Cyn.

Kaweahs

Kern River

Silliman Crest

Western Divide

Big Arroyo

Grant Grove

Black Rock Pass

Timber Gap

MINERAL KING

KENNETH REXROTH'S
MOUNTAIN POETRY

From In What Hour (1940)

CLIMBING MILESTONE MOUNTAIN, AUGUST 22, 1937

For a month now, wandering over the Sierras,
A poem had been gathering in my mind,
Details of significance and rhythm,
The way poems do, but still lacking a focus.
Last night I remembered the date and it all
Began to grow together and take on purpose.
        We sat up late while Deneb moved over the zenith
And I told Marie all about Boston, how it looked
That last terrible week, how hundreds stood weeping
Impotent in the streets that last midnight.
I told her how those hours changed the lives of thousands,
How America was forever a different place
Afterwards for many.
                In the morning
We swam in the cold transparent lake, the blue
Damsel flies on all the reeds like millions
Of narrow metallic flowers, and I thought
Of you behind the grille in Dedham, Vanzetti,
Saying, "Who would ever have thought we would make this history?"
Crossing the brilliant mile-square meadow
Illuminated with asters and cyclamen,
The pollen of the lodgepole pines drifting
With the shifting wind over it and the blue
And sulphur butterflies drifting with the wind,
I saw you in the sour prison light, saying,
"Goodbye comrade."

In the basin under the crest
Where the pines end and the Sierra primrose begins,
A party of lawyers was shooting at a whiskey bottle.
The bottle stayed on its rock, nobody could hit it.
Looking back over the peaks and canyons from the last lake,
The pattern of human beings seemed simpler
Than the diagonals of water and stone.
Climbing the chute, up the melting snow and broken rock,
I remembered what you said about Sacco,
How it slipped your mind and you demanded it be read into the
record.
Traversing below the ragged arête,
One cheek pressed against the rock
The wind slapping the other,
I saw you both marching in an army
You with the red and black flag, Sacco with the rattlesnake banner.
I kicked steps up the last snow bank and came
To the indescribably blue and fragrant
Polemonium and the dead sky and the sterile
Crystalline granite and final monolith of the summit.
These are the things that will last a long time, Vanzetti,
I am glad that once on your day I have stood among them.
Some day mountains will be named after you and Sacco.
They will be here and your name with them,
"When these days are but a dim remembering of the time
When man was wolf to man."
I think men will be remembering you a long time
Standing on the mountains
Many men, a long time, comrade.

NORTH PALISADE, THE END OF SEPTEMBER, 1939

The sun drops daily down the sky,
The long cold crawls near,
The aspen spills its gold in the air,
Lavish beyond the mind.
This is the last peak, the last climb.
New snow freckles the granite.
The imperious seasons have granted
Courage of a different kind.
Once more only in the smother
Of storm will the wary rope
Vanquish uncertain routes,
This year or another.
Once more only will the peak rise
Lucent above the dropping storm,
Skilled hand and steadfast foot accord
Victory of the brain and eye.
Practice is done, the barren lake
That mirrors this night's fire
Will hold unwinking unknown stars
In its unblemished glaze.

"Now winter nights enlarge
The number of our hours,"
They march to test their power,
We to betray their march.
Their rabbit words and weasel minds
Play at a losing game.
Ours is the unity of aim,
Theirs the diversity of pride.

Their victories on either side
Drive more deep the iron.
Ours is the victory to claim,
Ours is the peace to find.

HIKING ON THE COAST RANGE

> *On the Anniversary of the Killing of*
> *Sperry and Conderakias in the*
> *San Francisco General Strike*
> *Their Blood Spilled on the Pavement*
> *Of the Embarcadero*

The skirl of the kingfisher was never
More clear than now, nor the scream of the jay,
As the deer shifts her covert at a footfall;
Nor the butterfly tulip ever brighter
In the white spent wheat; nor the pain
Of a wasp stab ever an omen more sure;
The blood alternately dark and brilliant
On the blue and white bandana pattern.
This is the source of evaluation,
This minimal prince rupert's drop of blood;
The patellae suspended within it,
Leucocytes swimming freely between them,
The strands of fibrin, the mysterious
Chemistry of the serum; is alone
The measure of time, the measure of space,
The measure of achievement.
                                    There is no
Other source than this.

ON WHAT PLANET

Uniformly over the whole countryside
The warm air flows imperceptibly seaward;
The autumn haze drifts in deep bands
Over the pale water;
White egrets stand in the blue marshes;
Tamalpais, Diablo, St. Helena
Float in the air.
Climbing on the cliffs of Hunter's Hill
We look out over fifty miles of sinuous
Interpenetration of mountains and sea.

Leading up a twisted chimney,
Just as my eyes rise to the level
Of a small cave, two white owls
Fly out, silent, close to my face.
They hover, confused in the sunlight,
And disappear into the recesses of the cliff.

All day I have been watching a new climber,
A young girl with ash blonde hair
And gentle confident eyes.
She climbs slowly, precisely,
With unwasted grace.
While I am coiling the ropes,
Watching the spectacular sunset,
She turns to me and says, quietly,
"It must be very beautiful, the sunset,
On Saturn, with the rings and all the moons."

TOWARD AN ORGANIC PHILOSOPHY

Spring, Coast Range

The glow of my campfire is dark red and flameless,
The circle of white ash widens around it.
I get up and walk off in the moonlight and each time
I look back the red is deeper and the light smaller.
Scorpio rises late with Mars caught in his claw;
The moon has come before them, the light
Like a choir of children in the young laurel trees.
It is April; the shad, the hot headed fish,
Climbs the rivers; there is trillium in the damp canyons;
The foetid adder's tongue lolls by the waterfall.
There was a farm at this campsite once, it is almost gone now.
There were sheep here after the farm, and fire
Long ago burned the redwoods out of the gulch,
The Douglas fir off the ridge; today the soil
Is stony and incoherent, the small stones lie flat
And plate the surface like scales.
Twenty years ago the spreading gully
Toppled the big oak over onto the house.
Now there is nothing left but the foundations
Hidden in poison oak, and above on the ridge,
Six lonely, ominous fenceposts;
The redwood beams of the barn make a footbridge
Over the deep waterless creek bed;
The hills are covered with wild oats
Dry and white by midsummer.
I walk in the random survivals of the orchard.
In a patch of moonlight a mole
Shakes his tunnel like an angry vein;

Orion walks waist deep in the fog coming in from the ocean;
Leo crouches under the zenith.
There are tiny hard fruits already on the plum trees.
The purity of the apple blossoms is incredible.
As the wind dies down their fragrance
Clusters around them like thick smoke.
All the day they roared with bees, in the moonlight
They are silent and immaculate.

SPRING, SIERRA NEVADA

Once more golden Scorpio glows over the col
Above Deadman Canyon, orderly and brilliant,
Like an inspiration in the brain of Archimedes.
I have seen its light over the warm sea,
Over the coconut beaches, phosphorescent and pulsing;
And the living light in the water
Shivering away from the swimming hand,
Creeping against the lips, filling the floating hair.
Here where the glaciers have been and the snow stays late,
The stone is clean as light, the light steady as stone.
The relationship of stone, ice and stars is systematic and enduring;
Novelty emerges after centuries, a rock spalls from the cliffs,
The glacier contracts and turns grayer,
The stream cuts new sinuosities in the meadow,
The sun moves through space and the earth with it,
The stars change places.
                              The snow has lasted longer this year,
Than anyone can remember. The lowest meadow is a lake,
The next two are snowfields, the pass is covered with snow,
Only the steepest rocks are bare. Between the pass

And the last meadow the snowfield gapes for a hundred feet,
In a narrow blue chasm through which a waterfall drops,
Spangled with sunset at the top, black and muscular
Where it disappears again in the snow.
The world is filled with hidden running water
That pounds in the ears like ether;
The granite needles rise from the snow, pale as steel;
Above the copper mine the cliff is blood red,
The white snow breaks at the edge of it;
The sky comes close to my eyes like the blue eyes
Of someone kissed in sleep.
                              I descend to camp,
To the young, sticky, wrinkled aspen leaves,
To the first violets and wild cyclamen,
And cook supper in the blue twilight.
All night deer pass over the snow on sharp hooves,
In the darkness their cold muzzles find the new grass
At the edge of the snow.

FALL, SIERRA NEVADA

This morning the hermit thrush was absent at breakfast,
His place was taken by a family of chickadees;
At noon a flock of humming birds passed south,
Whirling in the wind up over the saddle between
Ritter and Banner, following the migration lane
Of the Sierra crest southward to Guatemala.
All day cloud shadows have moved over the face of the mountain,
The shadow of a golden eagle weaving between them
Over the face of the glacier.
At sunset the half-moon rides on the bent back of the Scorpion,

The Great Bear kneels on the mountain.
Ten degrees below the moon
Venus sets in the haze arising from the Great Valley.
Jupiter, in opposition to the sun, rises in the alpenglow
Between the burnt peaks. The ventriloquial belling
Of an owl mingles with the bells of the waterfall.
Now there is distant thunder on the east wind.
The east face of the mountain above me
Is lit with far off lightnings and the sky
Above the pass blazes momentarily like an aurora.
It is storming in the White Mountains,
On the arid fourteen-thousand-foot peaks;
Rain is falling on the narrow gray ranges
And dark sedge meadows and white salt flats of Nevada.
Just before moonset a small dense cumulus cloud,
Gleaming like a grape cluster of metal,
Moves over the Sierra crest and grows down the westward slope.
Frost, the color and quality of the cloud,
Lies over all the marsh below my campsite.
The wiry clumps of dwarfed whitebark pines
Are smoky and indistinct in the moonlight,
Only their shadows are really visible.
The lake is immobile and holds the stars
And the peaks deep in itself without a quiver.
In the shallows the geometrical tendrils of ice
Spread their wonderful mathematics in silence.
All night the eyes of deer shine for an instant
As they cross the radius of my firelight.
In the morning the trail will look like a sheep driveway,
All the tracks will point down to the lower canyon.
"Thus," says Tyndall, "the concerns of this little place
Are changed and fashioned by the obliquity of the earth's axis,

The chain of dependence which runs through creation,
And links the roll of a planet alike with the interests
Of marmots and men."

FALLING LEAVES AND EARLY SNOW

In the years to come they will say,
"They fell like the leaves
In the autumn of nineteen thirty-nine."
November has come to the forest,
To the meadows where we picked the cyclamen.
The year fades with the white frost
On the brown sedge in the hazy meadows,
Where the deer tracks were black in the morning.
Ice forms in the shadows;
Disheveled maples hang over the water;
Deep gold sunlight glistens on the shrunken stream.
Somnolent trout move through pillars of brown and gold.
The yellow maple leaves eddy above them,
The glittering leaves of the cottonwood,
The olive, velvety alder leaves,
The scarlet dogwood leaves,
Most poignant of all.

In the afternoon thin blades of cloud
Move over the mountains;
The storm clouds follow them;
Fine rain falls without wind.
The forest is filled with wet resonant silence.
When the rain pauses the clouds
Cling to the cliffs and the waterfalls.

In the evening the wind changes;
Snow falls in the sunset.
We stand in the snowy twilight
And watch the moon rise in a breach of cloud.
Between the black pines lie narrow bands of moonlight,
Glimmering with floating snow.
An owl cries in the sifting darkness.
The moon has a sheen like a glacier.

THE HEART UNBROKEN AND THE COURAGE FREE

It is late autumn, the end of Indian summer.
It was dry and warm all day, tonight it is cold.
In the light of the quarter moon the hoarfrost
Glows dimly on the dry long grass. A breeze starts
And stops and starts and makes waves on the hillside.
At the edge of the wild raspberry bushes
Four sooty spots bob about against the white frost.
They are rabbits with cold noses and cold toes.
Castor and Pollux blur in the first edge of fog.
Your breath is visible like fine autumn down,
Your eyes are polished with moonlight,
I look at them, they are the color of snow.

VALUE IN MOUNTAINS

1

There are those to whom value is a weapon,
Collectors of negatives and ascertables,

And those to whom value is horror,
Themselves collected by evaluation;
Who, recurrently dispossessed in each judgment,
Seizing or seized by presented fact,
Explode in a fury of discreet instants.

　　　Being is social in its immediacy,
Private in final implications;
Life is built of contact and dies secretly;
So existants live in history and die out
In fulfillment of individuals.

　　　Thus value is a food and not a weapon
Nor a challenge, process, not result, of judgment,
The morituri te salutamus
Of unique atomic realizations,
Enduring only in their eschatologies.

2

The shields of the peltasts of
The imagination quiver in the
Imagination the flourish
Of fire curves on the border
The eyelids gold and blue
The place of penumbras
Iris and pupil
Frosted or a star
Falling past Deneb
Past Aldebaran
Falling all night
Heavy as the songs
Arhythmic atonal

That drift with smoke
Across water
Or the cry rising
From between the buttes
The myrmidons
Of the imagination emerge
From stones
And sleep

3

Peace above this arch urged and bent, rising out
The frieze that not till high cold air in that time
Grown earthward vatic, incomprehensible
In trees inverted and copper galls of bloom,
Spoke death as speaking wrought; rhymed the butterflies;
Pared away rinds of thinking finer than thought;
Constructed tissues of a death of moments;
The translucent frieze of petals, of blue leaves,
Opposed blocked men with red granite molar hands;
Opposed the somnolescent will in its fact;
Bespoke the exfoliation of decay;
Compressed the angles at which the rods had leaned;
Stirred in the mind; settled the beams of passage;
Spoke death as fact, as fiat of becoming.
    The three shamans in their castle cubicies
Restored the prisms; replaced the discs and cubes;
Wrenched the taut lines welded in the cone of rays.
    Death spoke in atoms, speaking fine blown parsings
Of collected passage, syntax of the crumb.

4

He strikes the two rocks
He casts the four seeds
He marks in the dust
He draws three triangles
He burns the five feathers
He barks like the coyote
He paints his face white
He runs away

Has the arrow stood erect
The cones falling in cold water
All night the bell
And the delicate feet
A thousand leaves spinning
In the cube of ten thousand leaves
Or the cube that descends like a mist
The speaking voice will issue
From between immaculate red
And white alternates

The immediate fact
Is not perdurable
And speaking is being memory
The prisms falling in snow
Or web of air
And silver target
And the unique
Note
Of the stricken

A LESSON IN GEOGRAPHY

> *of Paradys ne can not I speken*
> *properly ffor I was not there*
> —Mandeville

The stars of the Great Bear drift apart
The Horse and the Rider together northeastward
Alpha and Omega asunder
The others diversely
There are rocks
On the earth more durable
Than the configurations of heaven
Species now motile and sanguine
Shall see the stars in new clusters
The beaches changed
The mountains shifted
Gigantic
Immobile
Floodlit
The faces appear and disappear
Chewing the right gum
Smoking the right cigarette
Buying the best refrigerator
The polished carnivorous teeth
Exhibited in approval
The lights
Of the houses
Draw together
In the evening dewfall on the banks
Of the Wabash
Sparkle discreetly

High on the road to Provo
Above the Salt Lake Valley
And
The mountain shaped like a sphinx
And
The mountain shaped like a finger
Pointing
On the first of April at eight o'clock
Precisely at Algol
There are rocks on the earth
And one who sleepless
Throbbed with the ten
Nightingales in the plum trees
Sleepless as Boötes stood over him
Gnawing the pillow
Sitting on the bed's edge smoking
Sitting by the window looking
One who rose in the false
Dawn and stoned
The nightingales in the garden
The heart pawned for wisdom
The heart
Bartered for knowledge and folly
The will troubled
The mind secretly aghast
The eyes and lips full of sorrow
The apices of vision wavering
As the flower spray at the tip of the windstalk
The becalmed sail
The heavy wordless weight
And now
The anguishing and pitiless file

Cutting away life
Capsule by capsule biting
Into the heart
The coal of fire
Sealing the lips
There are rocks on earth

And

In the Japanese quarter
A phonograph playing
"Moonlight on ruined castles"
Kōjō n'suki

And
The movement of the wind fish
Keeping time to the music
Sirius setting behind it
(The Dog has scented the sun)
Gold immense fish
Squirm in the trade wind
"Young Middle Western woman
In rut
Desires correspondent"
The first bright flower
Cynoglossum
The blue hound's tongue
Breaks on the hill
"The tide has gone down
Over the reef
I walk about the world
There is great

Wind and then rain"
"My life is bought and paid for
So much pleasure
For so much pain"
The folded fossiliferous
Sedimentary rocks end here
The granite batholith
Obtrudes abruptly
West of the fault line
Betelgeuse reddens
Drawing its substance about it
It is possible that a process is beginning
Similar to that which lifted
The great Sierra fault block
Through an older metamorphic range

(The Dog barks on the sun's spoor)

Now

The thought of death
Binds fast the flood of light
Ten years ago the snow falling
All a long winter night
I had lain waking in my bed alone
Turning my heavy thoughts
And no way might
Sleep
Remembering divers things long gone
Now
In the long day in the hour of small shadow
I walk on the continent's last western hill

And lie prone among the iris in the grass
My eyes fixed on the durable stone
That speaks and hears as though it were myself

ICE SHALL COVER NINEVEH

*But have you heard that, once upon a time, the city of Nineveh
stood where now one see the snow fields of the Gurgler Glacier?
I do not know myself whether it is true or not. They say that a
pilgrim came there and asked for bread. The people were miserly
and gave him only a sour crust. He rebuked them, and after his
departure, ice came and covered their city. I have heard that he was
one of the Three Wise Men. . . .*

*Austrian guns were mounted on the south peak of the Ortler,
and all the way down to the Payer hut we shall find the remains
of cables up which supplies were carried during the last weeks of
conflict. . . .*

*Tomorrow when you cross the Stelvio, you will see the galleries
and rock-cut trenches where many men lived and died. They were
mountain men like those cutting hay in the fields by which we
passed. There was no hatred in their hearts. Word came from the
cities that they must go out and kill.*

"Ice Shall Cover Nineveh" —J. Monroe Thorington
Sierra Club Bulletin, 1933

1

Distant on the meridian verges
And the soft equinoxes calling
Altair burns over the glacial
Pyramid it is evening

And the nighthawks pass over me
The great heron lifts from the water
And goes away the evening deepens
The stars come out and the owls under them
Dew falls between the mountains
And the Milky Way
Treeless and desolate
The lake lies under the last mountain
The moon rises and falling
Fringes of storm clouds blow over it
The wind barks in the cleft of the mountain
Sheep bells move in the valleys under me
The owls spiral close to the ground
The rain thickens and they go away
Lightning unwinds over the summit
I turn in sleep and speak aloud

2

Under the surgical and unnoticed
Sun now the gray rare
Condor goes over his swimming
Shadow over the matted alpine
Hemlock and gold trout waltz and
Flash in the volatile water
The mind splinters in attenuate air
The trail curls
Movement whistles into pain
The ache of bone the ache
Of immemorial blood
The sun goes under

The prostrate wood
The stars come over
The standing stone
Sacrifices and populations dissolve
We shall go away and not know when
Awakened at night and far away
In dense valleys bright life needles every clod
Neither fortified in dolmen nor reclined
In tumulus shall white throat and quick hand hide
Nor eye escape the rasp of powdering time

3

We would hear the sheep bells at night
And sometimes by day with the wind changing
But we spent two days hunting and calling
Because the tableland was full of wrinkles
With all sizes of lakes in them and covered
With stones the size and color of sheep
And then coming back from the pass
She saw in the dark his pipe glowing
And there he was standing against a big rock
A shadow on the pale stone watching the moon rise
Nothing would cook in water at that height
We lived for a week on fried fish bacon and flapjacks
Cooked over the cow dung of the herd
That had been through there two years back

4

The donations of this pattern
Intractable fact or hopeful
Platonism await the issue
Of type or archetype
Of being and existence
Desire anxious and faint
With expectation
Where the shrill
Gasp of spume the cord of water
Hangs from the arid granite
In the lacunae
Of space the interstices
Of the brain
Black wing and rose head
The yellow climbing bird
In the blue haze
Singing over the chasm
Or conversely who shall question
The donor who shall accept
With courtesy and illumination
The chill ground light
The clouds still orange and purple the sky
Unfathomed green
And dark cumbrous and busy
The bears in the huckleberries
Dampness rising from the meadow
The broken moon arriving
Ubiquitously through cloven rock
Or who shall sieve history
The adamant occasion

In bright obstinacy
From this obdurate avalanche

5

No ritual nor prayer shall let
Ungrind this molar precision of
Catastrophe nor shall bespeak
The stars of this vacant absolute
Tragedies swarm polarized between
Cerebrum and cerebellum infest
The wainscotting infest the medulla
Infest the endocrines
Light entering your eyes becomes
Brilliant with worms
All through the twilight air
Creeps a fog of nematodes
And no unguent
No moonlight wafer setting
In your final sky shall still
The roar of falling iron and stone
Falling with lightning and indifference
Beyond knowledge
And beyond interruption

6

Discover the apostleship of diffidence
As gently as bubbles circle out from
The foot of this waterfall and the sun

Declines as carefully find out the torc
And tension of this straight evangel as:
"Again they walk with me who once beside
Me walked the careful feet beside me waked
The meadow lark from the starlit white wheat"
(The song countered against a sun of three thousand suns
The inch-long blur of wings the humming bird
Hung in the fecund air) speak to the fractured
Moments of the aspen the military
Precise marsh iris intercolumniate
With fir and hemlock in smoke of twisted juniper
Memory ascends the mind
Goes up
Assents
The moon early after sundown
The emerald
Long mountain meadow
At the far end
Thirty
Red cattle
Below the peaks

7

A white body prone beneath meteors
And no moon in the moist night
Let a note ring in the immobile forest
The warped gong shuddering as the swung beam struck
Across the peaks clouds rise against the snow
The small eyes
Birds' feet

Flies' wings
And all voice still
Only the catheaded bird wavers through the sequoias
Only the bear snuffs shuffling and the marten
Stretches slit-eyed on a branch and sleeps
And the bronze body prone all day beneath
The hunting hawks all day soaring
Spirals in the narrow canyon sky
Falling suddenly to the moved grass
The two red-tailed hawks in the evening go off across the
    mountain
Let the gong speak in the impenetrable granite

8

The sudden eyes of gravid mice
The sunset on the blades of stone
The wide glow of a star falling across
Scorpio in the final altitudes
The crisp utterance of Spica in the evening
The light white in the pools water falling
Luminous through the bat quick air
Glory flashes once and is gone and we go
Stumbling but this is a slow omnivorous
Glory and endures as the mind shrivels
And the electric cancer of the eclipse
Crawls into the sky over the snow

9

Fear no more the eye of the sun
Nor the covert lemming's glance
You the invisible medusa
Have seen at twilight
And the waters wash on shell beaches
Pale blue in the long pale days
And the doe and the new fawn cross the bars
Of sunlight under the marsh lodgepole pines
Fear no more Polaris' sword
Nor the noiseless water vole
Nor any brilliant invertebrate
Nor molten nematode
Only the inorganic residues
Of your aspiration remain
Combed over by constellations
Vivisected by blades of wind
Fear no more the chill of the moon
No brisk rodent fear
Nor thirty years' dreams of falling
For frozen on the fixed final summit
Your mineral eyes reflect the gleaming
Perpetual fall of a cube of singular stone
Coursing its own parabola
Beyond imagination
Unto ages of ages

10

You return breathless having startled
Phoenixes in the arroyos and seen
On porphyry altars the pelican
Rend itself tirelessly and the creature
With uncounted eyes
And who now creaking in rust soft armor
Will bring this taper to the outer room
O the lost phalanxes the engulfed Gemini
Where the guillotine animal flies over the drowned lands
And the bleached heads turn incuriously
And no hand lifts
This Prometheus breeds his own eaglets
At first daybreak a voice opens crevices in the air
Fear no more
The horns of those gray hunters wind along
Ridges more inaccessible than dreams
Speak not let no word break
The stillness of this anguish
The omniscience of this vertigo
These lucent needles are fluent
In the gold of every memory
The past curls like wire

11

And now surprised by lunar mountain avatars
The avid eyes of gravid mice entice
Each icy nostrum of the zodiac
Sidelong on quivering feet the giants tread

The white Excaliburs the zero saws
The igneous granite pencils silvering
The plunge of light the coneys barking
The white lips speak and Danae
Danae writhing in the fluent metal
The camels the llamas the dogsleds the burros
Are loaded and go off in the white distance
And green over them the nova grows above the pass

12

Shall ask no more then forget the asker
Shall fail at laughter and in the dark
Go mumbling the parched gums fumbling the baggy heart
Bark with the mice in the rubbish bayed at by rats
The glaciers are senile and covered with dust but the
mountain cracks
The orange-red granite breaks and the long black slivers fall
Fine ice in the air and the stone blades falling and the
opening vault
The high milk-blue lake tipping over its edge in a mile-long
wavering waterfall
And for these weapons in what forge and from what steel
And for this wheat what winnowing floor what flail

From The Art of Worldly Wisdom (1949)

From IN THE MEMORY OF ANDRÉE REXROTH

c   *a time*

take one
from a pair a pair
from a quartet a quartet
from an
octet
the arrow through the octave
and the sun rising athwart
the ungloved thighs
the diamond refracted in honey
creep in thought
the minute spider creeps on the
eyeball the glass
rod swinging descends
ultimately to be
refracted in the pale
luminous solution
hair pulled by the wind
eyeballs flaked with light
the two princesses fall
from the ether of intensity
to the either of irrevocables
and the yellow
animal climbs the cascade in the secret
interior of the highest
mountain

From The Phoenix and the Tortoise (1944)

ANOTHER SPRING

The seasons revolve and the years change
With no assistance or supervision.
The moon, without taking thought,
Moves in its cycle, full, crescent, and full.

The white moon enters the heart of the river;
The air is drugged with azalea blossoms;
Deep in the night a pine cone falls;
Our campfire dies out in the empty mountains.

The sharp stars flicker in the tremulous branches;
The lake is black, bottomless in the crystalline night;
High in the sky the Northern Crown
Is cut in half by the dim summit of a snow peak.

O heart, heart, so singularly
Intransigent and corruptible,
Here we lie entranced by the starlit water,
And moments that should last forever

Slide unconsciously by us like water.

NIGHT BELOW ZERO

3 AM, the night is absolutely still;
Snow squeals beneath my skis, plumes on the turns.

I stop at the canyon's edge, stand looking out
Over the Great Valley, over the millions—
In bed, drunk, loving, tending mills, furnaces,
Alone, wakeful, as the world rolls in chaos.
The quarter moon rises in the black heavens—
Over the sharp constellations of the cities
The cold lies, crystalline and silent,
Locked between the mountains.

INVERSELY, AS THE SQUARE OF THEIR
DISTANCES APART

It is impossible to see anything
In this dark; but I know this is me, Rexroth,
Plunging through the night on a chilling planet.
It is warm and busy in this vegetable
Darkness where invisible deer feed quietly.
The sky is warm and heavy, even the trees
Over my head cannot be distinguished,
But I know they are knobcone pines, that their cones
Endure unopened on the branches, at last
To grow imbedded in the wood, waiting for fire
To open them and reseed the burned forest.
And I am waiting, alone, in the mountains,
In the forest, in the darkness, and the world
Falls swiftly on its measured ellipse.

It is warm tonight and very still.
The stars are hazy and the river—

Vague and monstrous under the fireflies—
Is hardly audible, resonant
And profound at the edge of hearing.
I can just see your eyes and wet lips.
Invisible, solemn, and fragrant,
Your flesh opens to me in secret.
We shall know no further enigma.
After all the years there is nothing
Stranger than this. We who know ourselves
As one doubled thing, and move our limbs
As deft implements of one fused lust,
Are mysteries in each other's arms.

———

At the wood's edge in the moonlight
We dropped our clothes and stood naked,
Swaying, shadow mottled, enclosed
In each other and together
Closed in the night. We did not hear
The whip-poor-will, nor the aspen's
Whisper; the owl flew silently
Or cried out loud, we did not know.
We could not hear beyond the heart.
We could not see the moving dark
And light, the stars that stood or moved,
The stars that fell. Did they all fall
We had not known. We were falling
Like meteors, dark through black cold
Toward each other, and then compact,
Blazing through air into the earth.

———

I lie alone in an alien
Bed in a strange house and morning
More cruel than any midnight
Pours its brightness through the window—
Cherry branches with the flowers
Fading, and behind them the gold
Stately baubles of the maple,
And behind them the pure immense
April sky and a white frayed cloud,
And in and behind everything,
The inescapable vacant
Distance of loneliness.

ANDRÉE REXROTH

died October 1940

Now once more gray mottled buckeye branches
Explode their emerald stars,
And alders smoulder in a rosy smoke
Of innumerable buds.
I know that spring again is splendid
As ever, the hidden thrush
As sweetly tongued, the sun as vital—
But these are the forest trails we walked together,
These paths, ten years together.
We thought the years would last forever,
They are all gone now, the days
We thought would not come for us are here.

Bright trout poised in the current—
The raccoon's track at the water's edge—
A bittern booming in the distance—
Your ashes scattered on this mountain—
Moving seaward on this stream.

ANDRÉE REXROTH

Purple and green, blue and white,
The Oregon river mouths
Slide into thick smoky darkness
As the turning cup of day
Slips from the whirling hemisphere.
And all that white long beach gleams
In white twilight as the lights
Come on in the lonely hamlets;
And voices of men emerge;
And dogs barking, as the wind stills.
Those August evenings are
Sixteen years old tonight and I
Am sixteen years older too—
Lonely, caught in the midst of life,
In the chaos of the world;
And all the years that we were young
Are gone, and every atom
Of your learned and disordered
Flesh is utterly consumed.

STRENGTH THROUGH JOY

Coming back over the col between
Isosceles Mountain and North Palisade,
I stop at the summit and look back
At the storm gathering over the white peaks
Of the Whitney group and the colored
Kaweahs. September, nineteen thirty-nine.
This is the last trip in the mountains
This autumn, possibly the last trip ever.
The storm clouds rise up the mountainside,
Lightning batters the pinnacles above me,
The clouds beneath the pass are purple
And I see rising through them from the valleys
And cities a cold, murderous flood,
Spreading over the world, lapping at the last
Inviolate heights; mud streaked yellow
With gas, slimy and blotched with crimson,
Filled with broken bits of steel and flesh,
Moving slowly with the blind motion
Of lice, spreading inexorably
As bacteria spread in tissues,
Swirling with the precise rapacity of starved rats.
I loiter here like a condemned man
Lingers over his last breakfast, his last smoke;
Thinking of those heroes of the war
Of human skill, foresight, endurance, and will;
The disinterested bravery,
The ideal combat of peace: Bauer
Crawling all night around his icecave
On snowbound Kanchenjunga, Tilman
And Shipton skylarking on Nanda Devi,

Smythe seeing visions on Everest,
The mad children of the Eigerwand—
What holidays will they keep this year?
Gun emplacements blasted in the rock;
No place for graves, the dead covered with quicklime
Or left in the snow till the spring thaw;
Machine gun duels between white robed ski troops,
The last screaming schusses marked with blood.
Was it for this we spent the years perfecting
The craft of courage? Better the corpse
Of the foolhardy, frozen on the Eiger
Accessible only to the storm,
Standing sentry for the avalanche.

INCARNATION

Climbing alone all day long
In the blazing waste of spring snow,
I came down with the sunset's edge
To the highest meadow, green
In the cold mist of waterfalls,
To a cobweb of water
Woven with innumerable
Bright flowers of wild iris;
And saw far down our fire's smoke
Rising between the canyon walls,
A human thing in the empty mountains.
And as I stood on the stones
In the midst of whirling water,
The whirling iris perfume
Caught me in a vision of you

More real than reality:
Fire in the deep curves of your hair,
Your hips whirled in a tango,
Out and back in dim scented light;
Your cheeks snow-flushed, the zithers
Ringing, all the crowded ski lodge
Dancing and singing; your arms
White in the brown autumn water,
Swimming through the fallen leaves,
Making a fluctuant cobweb
Of light on the sycamores;
Your thigh's exact curve, the fine gauze
Slipping through my hands, and you
Tense on the verge of abandon;
Your breasts' very touch and smell;
The sweet secret odor of sex.
Forever the thought of you,
And the splendor of the iris,
The crinkled iris petal,
The gold hairs powdered with pollen,
And the obscure cantata
Of the tangled water, and the
Burning impassive snowy peaks,
Are knotted together here.
This moment of fact and vision
Seizes immortality,
Becomes the person of this place.
The responsibility
Of love realized and beauty
Seen burns in a burning angel
Real beyond flower or stone.

From The Signature of All Things (1949)

LYELL'S HYPOTHESIS AGAIN

> *An Attempt to Explain the Former*
> *Changes of the Earth's Surface by*
> *Causes Now in Operation*
>   Subtitle of Lyell: *Principles of Geology*

The mountain road ends here,
Broken away in the chasm where
The bridge washed out years ago.
The first scarlet larkspur glitters
In the first patch of April
Morning sunlight. The engorged creek
Roars and rustles like a military
Ball. Here by the waterfall,
Insuperable life, flushed
With the equinox, sentient
And sentimental, falls away
To the sea and death. The tissue
Of sympathy and agony
That binds the flesh in its Nessus' shirt;
The clotted cobweb of unself
And self; sheds itself and flecks
The sun's bed with darts of blossom
Like flagellant blood above
The water bursting in the vibrant
Air. This ego, bound by personal
Tragedy and the vast
Impersonal vindictiveness

Of the ruined and ruining world,
Pauses in this immortality,
As passionate, as apathetic,
As the lava flow that burned here once;
And stopped here; and said, "This far
And no further." And spoke thereafter
In the simple diction of stone.

———

Naked in the warm April air,
We lie under the redwoods,
In the sunny lee of a cliff.
As you kneel above me I see
Tiny red marks on your flanks
Like bites, where the redwood cones
Have pressed into your flesh.
You can find just the same marks
In the lignite in the cliff
Over our heads. *Sequoia
Langsdorfii* before the ice,
And *sempervirens* afterwards,
There is little difference,
Except for all those years.

Here in the sweet, moribund
Fetor of spring flowers, washed,
Flotsam and jetsam together,
Cool and naked together,
Under this tree for a moment,
We have escaped the bitterness
Of love, and love lost, and love

Betrayed. And what might have been,
And what might be, fall equally
Away with what is, and leave
Only these ideograms
Printed on the immortal
Hydrocarbons of flesh and stone.

BLUES

The tops of the higher peaks
Of the Sierra Nevada
Of California are
Drenched in the perfume of
A flower which grows only there—
The blue *Polemonium*
Confertum eximium,
Soft, profound blue, like the eyes
Of impregnable innocence;
The perfume is heavy and
Clings thickly to the granite
Peaks, even in violent wind;
The leaves are clustered,
Fine dull green, sticky, and musky.
I imagine that the scent
Of the body of Artemis
That put Endymion to sleep
Was like this and her eyes had the
Same inscrutable color.
Lawrence was lit into death
By the blue gentians of Kore.
Vanzetti had in his cell

A bowl of tall blue flowers
From a New England garden.
I hope that when I need it
My mind can always call back
This flower to its hidden senses.

ANDRÉE REXROTH

MT. TAMALPAIS

The years have gone. It is spring
Again. Mars and Saturn will
Soon come on, low in the West,
In the dusk. Now the evening
Sunlight makes hazy girders
Over Steep Ravine above
The waterfalls. The winter
Birds from Oregon, robins
And varied thrushes, feast on
Ripe toyon and madrone
Berries. The robins sing as
The dense light falls.
                    Your ashes
Were scattered in this place. Here
I wrote you a farewell poem,
And long ago another,
A poem of peace and love,
Of the lassitude of a long
Spring evening in youth. Now
It is almost ten years since
You came here to stay. Once more,

The pussy willows that come
After the New Years in this
Outlandish land are blooming.
There are deer and raccoon tracks
In the same places. A few
New sand bars and cobble beds
Have been left where erosion
Has gnawed deep into the hills.
The rounds of life are narrow.
War and peace have passed like ghosts.
The human race sinks towards
Oblivion. A bittern
Calls from the same rushes where
You heard one on our first year
In the West; and where I heard
One again in the year
Of your death.

KINGS RIVER CANYON

My sorrow is so wide
I cannot see across it;
And so deep I shall never
Reach the bottom of it.
The moon sinks through deep haze,
As though the Kings River Canyon
Were filled with fine, warm, damp gauze.
Saturn gleams through the thick light
Like a gold, wet eye; nearby,
Antares glows faintly,
Without sparkle. Far overhead,

Stone shines darkly in the moonlight—
Lookout Point, where we lay
In another full moon, and first
Peered down into this canyon.
Here we camped, by still autumnal
Pools, all one warm October.
I baked you a bannock birthday cake.
Here you did your best paintings—
Innocent, wondering landscapes.
Very few of them are left
Anywhere. You destroyed them
In the terrible trouble
Of your long sickness. Eighteen years
Have passed since that autumn.
There was no trail here then.
Only a few people knew
How to enter this canyon.
We were all alone, twenty
Miles from anybody;
A young husband and wife,
Closed in and wrapped about
In the quiet autumn,
In the sound of quiet water,
In the turning and falling leaves,
In the wavering of innumerable
Bats from the caves, dipping
Over the odorous pools
Where the great trout drowsed in the evenings.

Eighteen years have been ground
To pieces in the wheels of life.
You are dead. With a thousand

Convicts they have blown a highway
Through Horseshoe Bend. Youth is gone,
That only came once. My hair
Is turning grey and my body
Heavier. I too move on to death.
I think of Henry King's stilted
But desolated *Exequy*,
Of Yuan Chen's great poem,
Unbearably pitiful;
Alone by the Spring river
More alone than I had ever
Imagined I would ever be,
I think of Frieda Lawrence,
Sitting alone in New Mexico,
In the long drought, listening
For the hiss of the milky Isar,
Over the cobbles, in a lost Spring.

From Beyond the Mountains (1951)

From HERMAIOS

I Chorus:

The twilight has gone like breath.

In the sharp starlight the snow
Stretches endlessly away
Into the dark at the foot
Of the mountains, like the white sands
On all the beaches of the sea.

The wind comes and goes with a sound
Like a vast concourse of people.

———

Kalliope:

I am tired of the long cold, too.
And this thin air burns my nostrils,
Parches my skin and dries my hair.
There's never enough to breathe here.
The air is too thin to sing with,
And poor stuff for the gulp of love.
Even the stars burn without oil,
Like burning icicles....

Snow. The wind is blowing the snow.
It's not living like fallen snow.
It's fine and dry like marble dust.
Soon it will drift over the roofs,
And seal us in for the winter.
I suppose it has a secret
Music, too. It has a sterile
Sort of geometry. I know
The one thin tune of its silence.
I don't find it interesting.

She goes out.

From BERENIKE

I Chorus:

The wind in the mountains has stopped.
The silence comes back like a thought.

The frozen water is still,
But the pulsating moonlight
Makes ripples in the clear ice.

Haunted by consequence, all
Existence is uneasy....

Berenike:

Demetrios
Is dead.

She points. Menander looks at him in silence for a while.

Menander:

He seems to be with friends.
They get along with each other.
        ... I wish I could
Touch them and say, "Live, run away,
Hide in the mountains. For thirty
Years you can eat mutton and loll
Beside meadow streams blowing
Grass whistles at the passing clouds."

Berenike:

He who buys a dried fish so that
He can set it free, does not know
The distinctions of life and death.

———————

The dance takes definition here.

I Chorus:

Light falls through the empty heaven.

Stars drift and rock on the waves of time.

The transparent earth curdles to stone.

Light floods the rock. Water is born
From stone. Air springs from the wave's spray.
Fire kindles in the light-filled air.

Light curdles in the virgin womb.

The earth turns to a crystal ball.
The child is at the gates. The waves
Of the endless sea grow still.

Light
Shines, a perfect disc reflected
In infinite calm.

Light narrows
To a point.

The point of light gives birth
To an illimitable sphere
Of rainbows flowing forever.

The dance closes during the next six lines.

II Chorus:

The star climbs near the zenith.
Soon it will stand above them,
Where they wait in the desert.

The whirling equinoxes
Close their term.

The Great Year ends.

The heavens begin again.
But we will not begin.

Time
Is all gone for the Greeks now.

From The Dragon and the Unicorn (1952)

TIME SPIRALS

Under the second moon the
Salmon come, up Tomales
Bay, up Papermill Creek, up
The narrow gorge to their spawning
Beds in Devil's Gulch. Although
I expect them, I walk by the
Stream and hear them splashing and
Discover them each year with
A start. When they are frightened
They charge the shallows, their immense
Red and blue bodies thrashing
Out of the water over
The cobbles; undisturbed, they
Lie in the pools. The struggling
Males poise and dart and recoil.
The females lie quiet, pulsing
With birth. Soon all of them will
Be dead, their handsome bodies
Ragged and putrid, half the flesh
Battered away by their great
Lust. I sit for a long time
In the chilly sunlight by
The pool below my cabin
And think of my own life—so much
Wasted, so much lost, all the
Pain, all the deaths and dead ends,
So very little gained after
It all. Late in the night I

Come down for a drink. I hear
Them rushing at one another
In the dark. The surface of
The pool rocks. The half moon throbs
On the broken water. I
Touch the water. It is black,
Frosty. Frail blades of ice form
On the edges. In the cold
Night the stream flows away, out
Of the mountain, towards the bay,
Bound on its long recurrent
Cycle from the sky to the sea.

MIRROR

The afternoon ends with red
Patches of light on the leaves
On the northeast canyon wall.
My tame owl sits serenely
On his dead branch. A foolish
Jay squalls and plunges at him.
He is ignored. The owl yawns
And stretches his wings. The jay
Flies away screaming with fright.
My king snake lies in inert
Curves over books and papers.
Even his tongue is still, but
His yellow eyes are judicial.
The mice move delicately
In the walls. Beyond the hills
The moon is up, and the sky

Turns to crystal before it.
The canyon blurs in half light.
An invisible palace
Of glass, full of transparent
People, settles around me.
Over the dim waterfall
The intense promise of light
Grows above the canyon's cleft.
A nude girl enters my hut,
With white feet, and swaying hips,
And fragrant sex.

Final passage of THE DRAGON AND THE UNICORN

... Off from the climbing road fall
Away folded shadows of
Mountains, range on moony range.
Under the waning moon the great
Valley like a hazy sea,
The town like the riding lights
Of fishing boats. The mountain
Peaks white and indistinct, their
Congruent tops merged in a high
Undulant horizon. Faint
Bells come up from the meadows.

The insecurity and
Ambiguity of modern
Culture is a reflection
Of the instability
Of the love relationship.

Art provides instruments of
Contemplation. Contemplation
Is the satisfaction of fulfilled
Love relationships, union with
The beloved object. If love is
Invalided, the whole fabric
Of the world culture crumbles.

Little Blue Lake—violet
Green swallows skimming above
Their reflections and dipping
To sip the water from their
Imaged beaks. Deep, deep and still,
Black and grey cliffs and white snow,
And the pale pure blue drowned ice.

Tara, the Power of Buddha;
Kali, the Power of Shiva;
Artemis, Apollo's sister;
The Wisdom of the Lord; the
Shekinah, Jehovah's Glory;
Mary the Mother of God;
Magdalene, the Bride of Christ;
Act and power, the twin lovers;
Each reflects the other like
The two chambers of the heart.

The lavabo of Pilate
Was the Graal of the Passover.

Once more we climb up the long
Gentle grade to Chagoopa

Plateau and look back, through the
Twisted foxtail pines growing
In the white talus, at the
Vast trough of Big Arroyo.
Again as always the Clark
Nutcrackers, grey, black and white,
Caw in the trees. Life repeats
Itself. We have camped here so
Many times by the shores of
Moraine Lake, the beautiful
Kaweah Peaks reflected
In the water, blue damsel
Flies on all the rushes.
In the evening, nighthawks
Will cry and dart through the air,
Dive, turn and swoop up again,
The twisting blades of their wings
Making a special growling roar
Like no other sound at all.
We will swim night and morning,
Catch golden trout in the creek,
See the water ouzel's nest
In the waterfall. Bear will
Bounce away from us as we
Wander between the open
Columns of the arid forest
Through the blue and white dwarf lupins.
In Sky Parlor Meadow there
Will be dozens of deer. The
Antlers of the bucks will look
Like dead branches above the
Tall rushes in the little lost

Marsh. The crimson bryanthus
And white Labrador tea will
Bloom by the lake as always.
In the evening crossing
The great meadow the sunset
On the water in the sedge
Will look like green and citron
Brocade, shot with copper and
Gold and blue—and the killdeer
Crying around us. And as
We come near camp, the nighthawks,
Those happy, happy birds,
Plunging over the lake again.
So the nighthawks cried over me
As I walked through smoky saffron
Twilights in the parks and long
Streets of Chicago in my
Entranced childhood. It is
Wise to keep the pattern of
Life clear and simple and filled
With beautiful and real things.
The round may be narrow enough.
The rounds of the world are narrower.

A truly radical, naïve,
Religious empiricism
Would describe all experience
In terms of its central fact.
The workings of the mind, the
Will, the physical and the
Transcendental worlds, would be seen
From the viewpoint of the

Contemplative immersed in
Contemplation. Reality
In a concourse of contemplatives.

Big Horn Plateau—four ravens,
Two hawks, one sandpiper, foxes
Barking in the rocks, the wool
Of wild sheep clinging to dead trees.
The voices of the thunder, all
The supernatural voices
Of the world, lightning striking
Continuously against the
Kaweahs, then the Kings-Kern peaks.
Here high above timberline,
Busy animacules swim
In the cold volatile water.
In the frosty moonlight the
Burro is restless. Coyotes
Howl close to camp all night long.

At the center of every
Universe, which flows from him
And back to him again is a
Contemplator; there are millions
Of universes, each with its
Contemplator, in a grain of sand.
Every entity, real or
Imagined, dust mote or hero
Of fiction, is one face of a
Contemplative—reality,
Their infinite conversation.

At twelve thousand feet, the perfume
Of the phlox is like a drug.
Far off, the foxtail forest
On Big Horn Plateau is orange
And black-green stubble. Clouds are
Rising in the distance beyond
Milestone and Thunder Mountains.
I glissade down the long snow bank
Of penitents to the shores
Of Tulainyo Lake, barren
As the moon. I break the thin
Crust of bubbly white ice and
Drink the black tasteless water.
I climb to the final ridge
And look out of the windows
In the fourteen thousand foot
Arête. At my feet are the
Bluest polemonium and
The most crimson primrose, and far
Away, the russet Inyo
Mountains rise through grey desert heat.
In the evening by the flaring
Campfire of timberline wood,
Full of pitch and incense, I read
Buddha's farewell to his harem
And watch the storm move in the night,
The lightning burning a fire
From peak to peak, far below me.

Christ—the good people are the
Bad people and the bad people
Are the good people. The world

Is going to be destroyed
Any minute now, so live.
And Buddha—at the center
Of being is the act of
Contemplation, unqualified,
Unique, unpredictable.

As long as we are lost
In the world of purpose
We are not free. I sit
In my ten foot square hut.
The birds sing. The bees hum.
The leaves sway. The water
Murmurs over the rocks.
The canyon shuts me in.
If I moved, Bashō's frog
Would splash in the pool.
All summer long the gold
Laurel leaves fell through space.
Today I was aware
Of a maple leaf floating
On the pool. In the night
I stare into the fire.
Once I saw fire cities,
Towns, palaces, wars,
Heroic adventures,
In the campfires of youth.
Now I see only fire.
My breath moves quietly.
The stars move overhead.
In the clear darkness
Only a small red glow

Is left in the ashes.
On the table lies a cast
Snakeskin and an uncut stone.

There is no need to assume
The existence of a god
Behind the community
Of persons, the community
Is the absolute. There is no
Future life because there is
No future. Reality
Is not conditioned by time,
Space, ignorance, grasping.
The shift from possibility
To consequence gives rise to
The convention of time. At
The heart of being is the act of
Contemplation, it is timeless.

Since Isis and Osiris
Many gods and goddesses
Have ridden the boats of
The sun and the moon. I stand
On the hill above my hut
And watch the sun set in the
Fog bank over the distant
Ocean. Shortly afterward
The moon rises, transparent
In the twilight above the
Mountain. There is nobody
In them this evening. I
Am sure they are empty, that

I am alone in the great
Void, where they journey, empty
Through the darkness and the light.

Deep in myself arise the rays
Called Artemis and Apollo,
Helios, Luna, Sun and Moon,
Flowing forever out into
The void, towards the unknown others.

The heavens and hells of man,
The gods and demons, the ghosts of
Superstition, are crude attempts;
The systems of philosophers,
The visions of religion,
Are more or less successful
Mythological descriptions
Of knowing, acting, loving—
You are Shiva, but you dream.

It is the dark of the moon.
Late at night, the end of Summer,
The Autumn constellations
Glow in the arid heaven.
The air smells of cattle, hay,
And dust. In the old orchard
The pears are ripe. The trees
Have sprouted from old rootstocks
And the fruit is inedible.
As I pass them I hear something
Rustling and grunting and turn
My light into the branches.

Two raccoons with acrid pear
Juice and saliva drooling
From their mouths, stare back at me,
Their eyes deep sponges of light.
They know me and do not run
Away. Coming up the road
Through the black oak shadows, I
See ahead of me, glinting
Everywhere from the dusty
Gravel, tiny points of cold
Blue light, like the sparkle of
Iron snow. I suspect what it is,
And kneel to see. Under each
Pebble and oak leaf is a
Spider, her eyes shining at
Me with my reflected light
Across immeasurable distance.

From In Defense of the Earth (1956)

A LIVING PEARL

At sixteen I came West, riding
Freights on the Chicago, Milwaukee
And St. Paul, the Great Northern,
The Northern Pacific. I got
A job as helper to a man
Who gathered wild horses in the
Mass drives in the Okanogan
And Horse Heaven country. The best
We culled out as part profit from
The drive, the rest went for chicken
And dog feed. We took thirty head
Up the Methow, up the Twisp,
Across the headwaters of Lake
Chelan, down the Skagit to
The Puget Sound country. I
Did the cooking and camp work.
In a couple of weeks I
Could handle the stock pretty well.
Every day we saddled and rode
A new horse. Next day we put a
Packsaddle on him. By the
Time we reached Marblemount
We considered them well broken.
The scissorbills who bought them
Considered them untamed mustangs
Of the desert. In a few weeks
They were peacefully pulling

Milk wagons in Sedro-Wooley.
We made three trips a season
And did well enough for the
Post-war depression.
Tonight,
Thirty years later, I walk
Out of the deserted miner's
Cabin in Mono Pass, under
The full moon and the few large stars.
The sidehills are piebald with snow.
The midnight air is suffused
With moonlight. As Dante says,
"It is as though a cloud enclosed
Me, lucid, dense, solid, polished,
Like a diamond forged by the sun.
We entered the eternal pearl,
Which took us as water takes
A ray of light, itself uncleft."
Fifteen years ago in this place,
I wrote a poem called, "Toward
An Organic Philosophy."
Everything is still the same,
And it differs very little
From the first mountain pass I
Crossed so long ago with the
Pintos and zebra duns and
Gunmetal roans and buckskins,
And splattered lallapaloosas,
The stocky wild ponies whose
Ancestors came with Coronado.
There are no horse bells tonight,
Only the singing of frogs

In the snow-wet meadows, the shrill
Single bark of a mountain
Fox, high in the rocks where the
Wild sheep move silently through the
Crystal moonlight. The same feelings
Come back. Once more all the awe
Of a boy from the prairies where
Lanterns move through the comfortable
Dark, along a fence, through a field,
Home; all the thrill of youth
Suddenly come from the flat
Geometrical streets of
Chicago, into the illimitable
And inhuman waste places
Of the Far West, where the mind finds
Again the forms Pythagoras
Sought, the organic relations
Of stone and cloud and flower
And moving planet and falling
Water. Marthe and Mary sleep
In their down bags, cocoons of
Mutual love. Half my life has
Been passed in the West, much of it
On the ground beside lonely fires
Under the summer stars, and in
Cabins where the snow drifted through
The pines and over the roof.
I will not camp here as often
As I have before. Thirty years
Will never come for me again.
"Our campfire dies out in the
Lonely mountains. The transparent

Moonlight stretches a thousand miles.
The clear peace is without end."
My daughter's deep blue eyes sleep
In the moon shadow. Next week
She will be one year old.

THE LIGHTS IN THE SKY ARE STARS

For Mary

HALLEY'S COMET

When in your middle years
The great comet comes again
Remember me, a child,
Awake in the summer night,
Standing in my crib and
Watching that long-haired star
So many years ago.
Go out in the dark and see
Its plume over water
Dribbling on the liquid night,
And think that life and glory
Flickered on the rushing
Bloodstream for me once, and for
All who have gone before me,
Vessels of the billion-year-long
River that flows now in your veins.

THE GREAT NEBULA OF ANDROMEDA

We get into camp after
Dark, high on an open ridge
Looking out over five thousand
Feet of mountains and mile
Beyond mile of valley and sea.
In the star-filled dark we cook
Our macaroni and eat
By lantern light. Stars cluster
Around our table like fireflies.
After supper we go straight
To bed. The night is windy
And clear. The moon is three days
Short of full. We lie in bed
And watch the stars and the turning
Moon through our little telescope.
Late at night the horses stumble
Around camp and I awake.
I lie on my elbow watching
Your beautiful sleeping face
Like a jewel in the moonlight.
If you are lucky and the
Nations let you, you will live
Far into the twenty-first
Century. I pick up the glass
And watch the Great Nebula
Of Andromeda swim like
A phosphorescent amoeba
Slowly around the Pole. Far
Away in distant cities
Fat-hearted men are planning
To murder you while you sleep.

THE HEART OF HERAKLES

Lying under the stars,
In the summer night,
Late, while the autumn
Constellations climb the sky,
As the Cluster of Hercules
Falls down the west
I put the telescope by
And watch Deneb
Move towards the zenith.
My body is asleep. Only
My eyes and brain are awake.
The stars stand around me
Like gold eyes. I can no longer
Tell where I begin and leave off.
The faint breeze in the dark pines,
And the invisible grass,
The tipping earth, the swarming stars
Have an eye that sees itself.

A MAZE OF SPARKS OF GOLD

Spring—the rain goes by, the stars
Shine pale beside the Easter
Moon. Scudding clouds, tossing leaves,
Whirl overhead. Blossoms fall
In the dark from the fragrant
Madrone trees. You lie beside
Me, luminous and still in sleep.
Overhead bees sleep in their
Tree. Beyond them the bees in

The Beehive in the Crab drift
Slowly past, a maze of points
Of fire. I've had ten times your
Years. Time holds us both fixed fast
Under the bright wasting stars.

A SWORD IN A CLOUD OF LIGHT

Your hand in mine, we walk out
To watch the Christmas Eve crowds
On Fillmore Street, the Negro
District. The night is thick with
Frost. The people hurry, wreathed
In their smoky breaths. Before
The shop windows the children
Jump up and down with spangled
Eyes. Santa Clauses ring bells,
Cars stall and honk. Streetcars clang.
Loud speakers on the lampposts
Sing carols, on juke boxes
In the bars Louis Armstrong
Plays "White Christmas." In the joints
The girls strip and grind and bump
To "Jingle Bells." Overhead
The neon signs scribble and
Erase and scribble again
Messages of avarice,
Joy, fear, hygiene, and the proud
Names of the middle classes.
The moon beams like a pudding.
We stop at the main corner

And look up, diagonally
Across, at the rising moon,
And the solemn, orderly
Vast winter constellations.
You say, "There's Orion!"
The most beautiful object
Either of us will ever
Know in the world or in life
Stands in the moonlit empty
Heavens, over the swarming
Men, women, and children, black
And white, joyous and greedy,
Evil and good, buyer and
Seller, master and victim,
Like some immense theorem,
Which, if once solved would forever
Solve the mystery and pain
Under the bells and spangles.
There he is, the man of the
Night before Christmas, spread out
On the sky like a true god
In whom it would only be
Necessary to believe
A little. I am fifty
And you are five. It would do
No good to say this and it
May do no good to write it.
Believe in Orion. Believe
In the night, the moon, the crowded
Earth. Believe in Christmas and
Birthdays and Easter rabbits.
Believe in all those fugitive

Compounds of nature, all doomed
To waste away and go out.
Always be true to these things.
They are all there is. Never
Give up this savage religion
For the blood-drenched civilized
Abstractions of the rascals
Who live by killing you and me.

PROTOPLASM OF LIGHT

How long ago
Frances and I took the subway
To Van Cortlandt Park. The people
All excited, small boys and
Cripples selling dark glasses.
We rushed to the open hills
North of the station as though
We'd be too late, and stood there
Hand in hand, waiting. Under
The trees the sun made little
Lunes of light through the bare branches
On the snow. The sky turned gray
And very empty. One by
One the stars came out. At last
The sun was only a thin
Crescent in our glasses with the
Bright planets nearby like watchers.
Then the great cold amoeba
Of crystal light sprang out
On the sky. The wind passed like

A silent crowd. The crowd sobbed
Like a passing wind. All the dogs
Howled. The silent protoplasm
Of light stood still in the black sky,
In its bowels, ringed with ruby
Fire, its stone-black nucleus.
Mercury, cold and dark like a
Fleck of iron, stood silent by it.
That was long ago.
Mary and I stand on the
Seashore and watch the sun sink
In the windy ocean. Layers
Of air break up the disc. It looks
Like a vast copper pagoda.
Spume blows past our faces, jellyfish
Pulse in the standing water,
Sprawl on the wet sand at our feet.
Twilight comes and all of the
Visible planets come out.
Venus first, and then Jupiter,
Mars and Saturn and finally
Mercury once more. Seals bark
On the rocks. I tell Mary
How Kepler never saw Mercury,
How, as he lay dying it shone
In his window, too late for him
To see. The mysterious
Cone of light leans up from the
Horizon into the pale sky.
I say, "Nobody knows what
It is or even where it is.
Maybe it is the great cloud

Of gas around the sun which
You will see some day if you
Are lucky. It stands out only
During an eclipse. I saw it
Long ago."

BLOOD ON A DEAD WORLD

A blowing night in late fall,
The moon rises with a nick
In it. All day Mary has
Been talking about the eclipse.
Every once in a while I
Go out and report on the
Progress of the earth's shadow.
When it is passing the half,
Marthe and Mary come out
And we stand on the corner
In the first wisps of chilling
Fog and watch the light go out.
Streamers of fog reach the moon,
But never quite cover it.
We have explained with an orange,
A grapefruit, and a lamp, not
That we expect a four
Year old child to understand—
Just as a sort of ritual
Duty. But we are surprised.
"The earth's shadow is like blood,"
She says. I tell her the Indians
Called an eclipse blood on the moon.

"Is it all the blood on the earth
Makes the shadow that color?"
She asks. I do not answer.

TIME IS THE MERCY OF ETERNITY

Time is divided into
Seconds, minutes, hours, years,
And centuries. Take any
One of them and add up its
Content, all the world over.
One division contains much
The same as any other.
What can you say in a poem?
Past forty, you've said it all.
The dwarf black oak grows out of
The cliff below my feet. It
May be two hundred years old,
Yet its trunk is no bigger
Than my wrist, its crown does not
Come to my shoulder. The late
Afternoon sun behind it
Fills its leaves with light like
A gem tree, like the wishing
Tree of jewels in the Eastern
Stories. Below it the cliff
Falls sheer away five hundred
Feet to a single burnt pine,
And then another thousand
Feet to a river, noisy
In spate. Off beyond it stretches

Shimmering space, then fold on
Dimmer fold of wooded hills,
Then, hardly visible in
The pulsating heat, the flat
Lands of the San Joaquin Valley,
Boiling with life and trouble.
The pale new green leaves twinkle
In the rising air. A blue
Black, sharp-beaked, sharp-crested jay
Rests for a moment amongst
Them and then plunges off, down
Through the hazy June afternoon.
Far away the writhing city
Burns in a fire of transcendence
And commodities. The bowels
Of men are wrung between the poles
Of meaningless antithesis.
The holiness of the real
Is always there, accessible
In total immanence. The nodes
Of transcendence coagulate
In you, the experiencer,
And in the other, the lover.
When the first blooms come on the
Apple trees, and the spring moon
Swims in immeasurable
Clear deeps of palpable light,
I sit by the waterfall.
The owls call, one beyond the
Other, indefinitely
Away into the warm night.
The moist black rocks gleam faintly.

The curling moss smells of wet life.
The waterfall is a rope
Of music, a black and white
Spotted snake in the moonlit
Forest. The thighs of the goddess
Close me in. The moon lifts into
The cleft of the mountains and a
Cloud of light pours around me like
Blazing perfume. When the moon has
Passed on and the owls are loud in
My ears again, I kneel and drink
The cold, sweet, twisting water.

All day clouds drift up the canyon.
By noon the high peaks are hidden.
Thunder mutters in the distance.
Suddenly the canyon is gone.
My camp on its narrow ledge is
Isolated in swirling mist.
Even the nearby pines grow dim,
And recede into the grayness.
Yellow lightning bursts, like fire through
Smoke, and sets all the mist aglow.
Thunder explodes under my feet.
The rain pours hissing through the
Pine needles. White hailstones fall
Awry between the red pine trunks.
They rattle on my tent. I catch
Some and watch them melt in my hand.
As evening comes, birds ruffle
Their feathers, and fly gingerly
From branch to branch, and sing a few

Notes, while through the orange twilight
Fall green, widely spaced drops of rain.

For three days the clouds have piled up,
And rain has circled the mountains.
For a while it will fall over
Black Rock Pass, and then move across
To the red Kaweahs, and then
On to the white Whitney Range. But
Here by the lake it does not fall,
And the air grows more oppressive.
I swim lazily. Even the
Water seems to be heavier.
The air is full of mosquitoes.
After a listless lunch, I sit
On the bank reading the wise poems
Of Charles Cros. Suddenly the wind
Rises. The tent flaps noisily.
Twigs and dust and pine needles fly
In all directions. Then the wind
Drops and the rain falls on the lake.
The drops chime against the ripples
Like the Japanese glass wind bells
I loved so much as a child.
The rain is gone in an hour.
In the clear evening freshness,
I hear the bell on my donkey,
In his meadow, a mile away.
Nighthawks cry overhead and dive,
Thrumming their wings as they turn.
A deer comes down to the water.
The high passes are closed with snow.

I am the first person in this season.
No one comes by. I am alone
In the midst of a hundred mountains.

Five o'clock, mid-August evening,
The long sunlight is golden
On the deep green grass and bright
Red flowers of the meadow.
I stop where a meander
Of the brook forms a deep pool.
The water is greenish brown,
But perfectly transparent.
A small dense cloud of hundreds
Of midges, no bigger than
My head, hovers over it.
On the bank are two small frogs.
In the water are beetles,
Hydras, water bugs, larvae
Of several insects. On
The surface are water boatmen.
I realize that the color
Of the water itself is
Due to millions of active
Green flecks of life. It is like
Peering into an inkspot,
And finding yourself staring
Out into the Milky Way.
The deep reverberation
Of my identity with
All this plenitude of life
Leaves me shaken and giddy.
I step softly across the

Meadows as the deer lift their
Antlers and idly watch me.

Here on this high plateau where
No one ever comes, beside
This lake filled with mirrored mountains,
The hours and days and weeks
Go by without variation.
Even the rare storms pass over
And empty themselves on the peaks.
There are no fish in the water.
There are few deer or bear in the woods.
Only the bright blue damsel flies
On the reeds in the daytime,
And the nighthawks overhead
In the evening. Suspended
In absolutely transparent
Air and water and time, I
Take on a kind of crystalline
Being. In this translucent
Immense here and now, if ever,
The form of the person should be
Visible, its geometry,
Its crystallography, and
Its astronomy. The good
And evil of my history
Go by. I can see them and
Weigh them. They go first, with all
The other personal facts,
And sensations, and desires.
At last there is nothing left
But knowledge, itself a vast

Crystal encompassing the
Limitless crystal of air
And rock and water. And the
Two crystals are perfectly
Silent. There is nothing to
Say about them. Nothing at all.

MARY AND THE SEASONS

DRY AUTUMN

In the evening, just before
Sunset, while we were cooking
Supper, we heard dogs, high on
The west ridge, running a deer.
With unbelievable speed
They quartered down the hillside,
Crossed the gulch, climbed the east ridge
And circled back above us.
As they rushed down again, I
Ran to catch them. The barking
Stopped when they reached the creek bed.
As I came near I could hear
The last terrified bleating
Of a fawn. By the time I
Got there it was already dead.
When the dogs caught sight of me,
They scurried guiltily away.
The fawn was not torn. It had
Died of fear and exhaustion.

My dearest, although you are
Still too young to understand,
At this moment horrible
Black dogs with eyes of fire and
Long white teeth and slavering
Tongues are hunting you in the dark
Mountains to eat your tender heart.

SPRING RAIN

The smoke of our campfire lowers
And coagulates under
The redwoods, like low-lying
Clouds. Fine mist fills the air. Drops
Rattle down from all the leaves.
As the evening comes on
The treetops vanish in fog.
Two saw-whet owls utter their
Metallic sobbing cries high
Overhead. As it gets dark
The mist turns to rain. We are
All alone in the forest.
No one is near us for miles.
In the firelight mice scurry
Hunting crumbs. Tree toads cry like
Tiny owls. Deer snort in the
Underbrush. Their eyes are green
In the firelight like balls of
Foxfire. This morning I read
Mei Yao Chen's poems, all afternoon
We walked along the stream through

Woods and meadows full of June
Flowers. We chased frogs in the
Pools and played with newts and young
Grass snakes. I picked a wild rose
For your hair. You brought
New flowers for me to name.
Now it is night and our fire
Is a red throat open in
The profound blackness, full of
The throb and hiss of the rain.

AUTUMN RAIN

Two days ago the sky was
Full of mares' tails. Yesterday
Wind came, bringing low cigar
Shaped clouds. At midnight the rain
Began, the first fine, still rain
Of autumn. Before the rain
The night was warm, the sky hazy.
We lay in the field and watched
The glowing October stars,
Vega, Deneb, Altair, high,
Hercules and the Crown setting,
The Great Nebula distinct
Through the haze. Every owl
In the world called and made love
And scolded. Once in a while
We would see one on the sky,
Cruising, on wings more silent
Than silence itself, low over

The meadow. The air thickened.
The stars grew dim and went out.
The owls stopped crying in the wood.
Then the rain came, falling so
Gently on the tent we did
Not notice until a slight
Breeze blew it in on our faces.
At dawn it was still raining.
It cleared as we cooked breakfast.
We climbed through tatters of cloud
To the east ridge and walked through
The dripping, sparkling fir forest.
In the meadow at the summit
We ate lunch in the pale sun,
Ever so slightly cooler,
And watched the same long autumn
Mares' tails and came back down the
Steep rocks through the soaking ferns.

CLEAR AUTUMN

This small flat clearing is not
Much bigger than a large room
In the steep narrow canyon.
On every side the slender
Laurel trunks shut us in close.
High on the southern sidehill
Patches of sunlight filter
Through the fir trees. But the sun
Will not come back here until
Winter is past. New-fallen

Leaves shine like light on the floor.
The air hums with low-flying
Insects, too weakened to rise.
The stream has stopped. Underground,
A trickle seeps from pool to pool.
All the summer birds have gone.
Only woodpeckers and jays
And juncos have stayed behind.
Soon the rains will start, and then
Fine, silent, varied thrushes
Will come from the dark rain forests
Of the Northwest, but not yet.
We climb to the long west ridge
That looks out on the ocean
And eat lunch at a high spring
Under the rocks at the top.
Holstein calves cluster around
And watch us impassively.
No wind moves in the dry grass.
The sky and the distant sea,
The yellow hills, stretching away,
Seem seen in a clouded mirror.
Buzzards on the rising air
Float without moving a wing.
Jet bombers play at killing
So high overhead only
Long white scrawls can be seen, the
Graffiti of genocide.
The planes are invisible.
Away from the sun the air
Glitters with millions of glass
Needles, falling from the zenith.

It is as though oxygen
And nitrogen were being
Penetrated and replaced
By some shining chemical.
It is the silk of a swarm
Of ballooning spiders, flashes
Of tinsel and drifting crystal
In the vast rising autumn air.
When we get back everything
Is linked with everything else
By fine bright strands of spun glass,
The golden floor of October,
Brilliant under a gauze of light.

SNOW

Low clouds hang on the mountain.
The forest is filled with fog.
A short distance away the
Giant trees recede and grow
Dim. Two hundred paces and
They are invisible. All
Day the fog curdles and drifts.
The cries of the birds are loud.
They sound frightened and cold. Hour
By hour it grows colder.
Just before sunset the clouds
Drop down the mountainside. Long
Shreds and tatters of fog flow
Swiftly away between the
Trees. Now the valley below

Is filled with clouds like clotted
Cream and over them the sun
Sets, yellow in a sky full
Of purple feathers. After dark
A wind rises and breaks branches
From the trees and howls in the
Treetops and then suddenly
Is still. Late at night I wake
And look out of the tent. The
Clouds are rushing across the
Sky and through them is tumbling
The thin waning moon. Later
All is quiet except for
A faint whispering. I look
Out. Great flakes of wet snow are
Falling. Snowflakes are falling
Into the dark flames of the
Dying fire. In the morning the
Pine boughs are sagging with snow,
And the dogwood blossoms are
Frozen, and the tender young
Purple and citron oak leaves.

ANOTHER TWILIGHT

Far out across the Great Valley
The sun sets behind the Coast Range.
The distant mountains mingle
With the haze of the valley,
Purple folded into purple.
Over them the evening

Turns orange and green, the white fire
Of Venus and the transparent
Crescent moon. Venus is caught
In the Crab's claws, the moon creeps
Between the Virgin's open thighs.
Bats dodge and squeak between the trees.
A velvety, chocolate-colored
Bear comes and begs for food. Two
Gray and orange foxes quarter
Over the ground below camp,
Searching for scraps. Their cubs
Peek out from the manzanita.

From Natural Numbers (1964)

HOMER IN BASIC

Glitter of Nausicaä's
Embroideries, flashing arms,
And heavy hung maiden hair;
Doing the laundry, the wind
Brisk in the bright air
Of the Mediterranean day.
Odysseus, hollow cheeked,
Wild eyed, bursts from the bushes.
Mary sits by the falling
Water reading Homer while
I fish for mottled brook trout
In the sun mottled riffles.
They are small and elusive.
The stream is almost fished out.
Water falls through shimmering
Panelled light between the red
Sequoias, over granite
And limestone, under green ferns
And purple lupin. Time was
I caught huge old trout in these
Pools and eddies. These are three
Years old at the very most.
Mary is seven. Homer
Is her favorite author.
It took me a lifetime of
Shames and wastes to understand
Homer. She says, "Aren't those gods

Terrible? All they do is
Fight like those angels in Milton,
And play tricks on the poor Greeks
And Trojans. I like Aias
And Odysseus best. They are
Lots better than those silly
Gods." Like the ability
To paint, she will probably
Outgrow this wisdom. It too
Will wither away as she
Matures and a whole lifetime
Will be spent getting it back.
Now she teaches Katharine
The profound wisdom of seven
And Katharine responds with
The profound nonsense of three.
Grey-haired in granite mountains,
I catch baby fish. Ten fish,
And Homer, and two little
Girls pose for a picture by
The twenty foot wide, cinnamon
Red trunk of a sequoia.
As I snap the camera,
It occurs to me that this
Tree was as big as the pines
Of Olympus, not just before
Homer sang, but before Troy
Ever fell or Odysseus
Ever sailed from home.

FISH PEDDLER AND COBBLER

Always for thirty years now
I am in the mountains in
August. For thirty Augusts
Your ghosts have stood up over
The mountains. That was nineteen
Twenty-seven. Now it is
Nineteen fifty-seven. Once
More after thirty years I
Am back in the mountains of
Youth, back in the Gros Ventres,
The broad park-like valleys and
The tremendous cubical
Peaks of the Rockies. I learned
To shave hereabouts, working
As cookee and night wrangler.
Nineteen twenty-two, the years
Of revolutionary
Hope that came to an end as
The iron fist began to close.
No one electrocuted me.
Nothing happened. Time passed.
Something invisible was gone.
We thought then that we were the men
Of the years of the great change,
That we were the forerunners
Of the normal life of mankind.
We thought that soon all things would
Be changed, not just economic
And social relationships, but
Painting, poetry, music, dance,

Architecture, even the food
We ate and the clothes we wore
Would be ennobled. It will take
Longer than we expected.
These mountains are unchanged since
I was a boy wandering
Over the West, picking up
Odd jobs. If anything they are
Wilder. A moose cow blunders
Into camp. Beavers slap their tails
On their sedgy pond as we fish
From on top of their lodge in the
Twilight. The horses feed on bright grass
In meadows full of purple gentian,
And stumble through silver dew
In the full moonlight.
The fish taste of meadow water.
In the morning on far grass ridges
Above the red rim rock wild sheep
Bound like rubbers balls over the
Horizon as the noise of camp
Begins. I catch and saddle
Mary's little golden horse,
And pack the first Decker saddles
I've seen in thirty years. Even
The horse bells have a different sound
From the ones in California.
Canada jays fight over
The last scraps of our pancakes.
On the long sandy pass we ride
Through fields of lavender primrose
While lightning explodes around us.

For lunch Mary catches a two pound
Grayling in the whispering river.
No fourteen thousand foot peaks
Are named Sacco and Vanzetti.
Not yet. The clothes I wear
Are as unchanged as the Decker
Saddles on the pack horses.
America grows rich on the threat of death.
Nobody bothers anarchists anymore.
Coming back we lay over
In Ogden for ten hours.
The courthouse square was full
Of miners and lumberjacks and
Harvest hands and gandy dancers
With broken hands and broken
Faces sleeping off cheap wine drunks
In the scorching heat, while tired
Savage eyed whores paraded the street.

From AIR AND ANGELS

MAROON BELLS

How can I love you more than
The silver whistle of the
Coney in the rocks loves you?
How can I love you better
Than the blue of the bluebells
By the waterfall loves you?
Eater of moonlight, drinker
Of brightness, feet of jewels

On the mountain, velvet feet
In the meadow grass, darkness
Braided with wild roses, wild
Mare of all the horizons ...
A far away tongue speaks in
The time that fills me like a
Tongue in a bell falling
Out of all the towers of space.
Eyes wide, nostrils distended,
We drown in secret happy
Oceans we trade in broad daylight.
O my girl, mistress of all
Illuminations and all
Commonplaces, I love you
Like the air and the water
And the earth and the fire and
The light love you and love you.

From One Hundred Poems from the Chinese
(1956)

WINTER DAWN

The men and beasts of the zodiac
Have marched over us once more.
Green wine bottles and red lobster shells,
Both emptied, litter the table.
"Should auld acquaintance be forgot?" Each
Sits listening to his own thoughts,
And the sound of cars starting outside.
The birds in the eaves are restless,
Because of the noise and light. Soon now
In the winter dawn I will face
My fortieth year. Borne headlong
Toward the long shadows of sunset
By the headstrong, stubborn moments,
Life whirls past like drunken wildfire.

Tu Fu

A RESTLESS NIGHT IN CAMP

In the penetrating damp
I sleep under the bamboos,
Under the penetrating
Moonlight in the wilderness.
The thick dew turns to fine mist.
One by one the stars go out.
Only the fireflies are left.

Birds cry over the water.
War breeds its consequences.
It is useless to worry,
Wakeful while the long night goes.

                        Tu Fu

SOUTH WIND

The days grow long, the mountains
Beautiful. The south wind blows
Over blossoming meadows.
Newly arrived swallows dart
Over the steaming marshes.
Ducks in pairs drowse on the warm sand.

                        Tu Fu

From One Hundred More Poems from the Chinese (1970)

A MOUNTAIN SPRING

There is a brook in the mountains,
Nobody I ask knows its name.
It shines on the earth like a piece
Of the sky. It falls away
In waterfalls, with a sound
Like rain. It twists between rocks
And makes deep pools. It divides
Into islands. It flows through
Calm reaches. It goes its way
With no one to mind it. The years
Go by, its clear depths never change.

Ch'u Ch'uang I

AUTUMN TWILIGHT IN THE MOUNTAINS

In the empty mountains after the new rain
The evening is cool. Soon it will be Autumn.
The bright moon shines between the pines.
The crystal stream flows over the pebbles.
Girls coming home from washing in the river
Rustle through the bamboo grove.
Lotus leaves dance behind the fisherman's boat.
The perfumes of Spring have vanished
But my guests will long remember them.

Wang Wei

SNOW ON LOTUS MOUNTAIN

Sunset. Blue peaks vanish in dusk.
Under the Winter stars
My lonely cabin is covered with snow.
I can hear the dogs barking
At the rustic gate.
Through snow and wind
Someone is coming home.

          Liu Ch'ang Ch'ing

AMONGST THE CLIFFS

The path up the mountain is hard
To follow through the tumbled rocks.
When I reach the monastery
The bats are already flying.
I go to the guest room and sit
On the steps. The rain is over.
The banana leaves are broad.
The gardenias are in bloom.
The old guest master tells me
There are ancient paintings on the
Walls. He goes and gets a light
I see they are incomparably
Beautiful. He spreads my bed
And sweeps the mat. He serves me
Soup and rice. It is simple
Food but nourishing. The night
Goes on as I lie and listen
To the great peace. Insects chirp

And click in the stillness. The
Pure moon rises over the ridge
And shines in my door. At daybreak
I get up alone. I saddle
My horse myself and go my way.
The trails are all washed out.
I go up and down, picking my
Way through storm clouds on the mountain.
Red cliffs, green waterfalls, all
Sparkle in the morning light.
I pass pines and oaks ten men
Could not reach around. I cross
Flooded streams. My bare feet stumble
On the cobbles. The water roars.
My clothes whip in the wind. This
Is the only life where a man
Can find happiness. Why do I
Spend my days bridled like a horse
With a cruel bit in his mouth?
If I only had a few friends
Who agreed with me we'd retire
To the mountains and stay till our lives end.

                                        Han Yu

WHEN WILL I BE HOME?

When will I be home? I don't know.
In the mountains, in the rainy night,
The Autumn lake is flooded.
Someday we will be back together again.
We will sit in the candlelight by the West window,

And I will tell you how I remembered you
Tonight on the stormy mountain.

Li Shang Yin

IN THE MOUNTAINS AS AUTUMN BEGINS

Cold air drains down from the peaks.
Frost lies all around my cabin.
The trees are bare. Weak sunlight
Shines in my window. The pond
Is full and still. The water
Is motionless. I watch the
Gibbons gather fallen fruit.
All night I hear the deer stamping
In the dry leaves. My old harp
Soothes all my trouble away.
The clear voice of the waterfall
In the night accompanies my playing.

Wen T'ing Yen

From Gödel's Proof (1965)

YIN AND YANG

It is spring once more in the Coast Range
Warm, perfumed, under the Easter moon.
The flowers are back in their places.
The birds back in their usual trees.
The winter stars set in the ocean.
The summer stars rise from the mountains.
The air is filled with atoms of quicksilver.
Resurrection envelops the earth.
Geometrical, blazing, deathless,
Animals and men march through heaven,
Pacing their secret ceremony.
The Lion gives the moon to the Virgin.
She stands at the crossroads of heaven,
Holding the full moon in her right hand,
A glittering wheat ear in her left.
The climax of the rite of rebirth
Has ascended from the underworld
Is proclaimed in light from the zenith.
In the underworld the sun swims
Between the fish called Yes and No.

From The Heart's Garden, The Garden's Heart (1967)

A SONG AT THE WINEPRESSES

for Gary Snyder

It is the end of the grape
Harvest. How amiable
Thy dwellings, the little huts
Of branches in the vineyards
Where the grape pickers rested.
Adieu, paniers, vendanges sont faites.
Five months have passed. Here am I—
Another monastery
Garden, another waterfall,
And another religion,
Perched on the mountain's shoulder,
Looking out over fogbound
Santa Barbara. Cactus
And stone make up the garden,
At its heart a heavy cross.
Off behind the monastery,
Deep in the canyon, a cascade
Of living water, green and white,
Breaks the arid cliffs, twisting
Through yellow sandstone boulders,
Sycamores, canyon oaks, laurels,
Toyonberries, maples, pines.
Buzzards dream on the wing, high
On the rising morning air.

A canyon wren sings on a dead
Yucca stem. Over a high rock
Across the stream, a bobcat
Peeks at me for a moment.
A panting doe comes down to drink.
And then the same water ouzel
I just saw above Kyoto.
Passing through the dry valley
Of gum trees, they make it a place
Of springs, and the pools are filled
With water. Deep calls to deep
In the voice of the cataracts.
Loving kindness watches over
Me in the daytime and a song
Guards me all through the starlit night.
Altair and Vega are at
The zenith in the evening.
The cowboy has gone back
Across the Cloudy River.
The weaving girl is pregnant
With another year. The magpie
Wing bridge of dreams has dissolved.
The new wine dreams in the vat.
Low over the drowsy sea,
The sea goat moves towards the sun.
Richard of St. Victor says,
"Contemplation is a power
That coordinates the vast
Variety of perception
Into one all embracing
Insight, fixed in wonder on
Divine things—admiration,

Awe, joy, gratitude—singular,
Insuperable, but at rest."
The sparrow has found her a home,
The swallow a nest for herself,
Where she may raise her brood.
When we have tea in the loggia,
Rusty brown California towhees
Pick up crumbs around our feet.
The towhees were pets of the Indians.
They are still to be found on
The sites of old rancherías,
Waiting for the children to
Come and feed them acorn cakes.
Just so the swallows still nest
In the eaves of all the buildings
On the site of the vanished
Temple in Jerusalem.
Above us from the rafters
Of the loggia hang two wooden
Mexican angels; on their rumps
Are birds' nests. The Autumn sun
Is a shield of gold in heaven.
The hills wait for the early rain
To clothe them in blessings of flowers.
It is the feast of Raphael
The archangel, and Tobit
And the faithful dog.

                Mt. Calvary, Santa Barbara, 1967

From Love is the Art of Time (1974)

YOUR BIRTHDAY IN THE CALIFORNIA
MOUNTAINS

A broken moon on the cold water,
And wild geese crying high overhead,
The smoke of the campfire rises
Toward the geometry of heaven—
Points of light in the infinite blackness.
I watch across the narrow inlet
Your dark figure comes and goes before the fire.
A loon cries out on the night bound lake.
Then all the world is silent with the
Silence of autumn waiting for
The coming of winter. I enter
The ring of firelight, bringing to you
A string of trout for our dinner.
As we eat by the whispering lake,
I say, "Many years from now we will
Remember this night and talk of it."
Many years have gone by since then, and
Many years again. I remember
That night as though it was last night,
But you have been dead for thirty years.

HAPAX

THE SAME POEM OVER AND OVER

Holy Week. Once more the full moon
Blooms in deep heaven
Like a crystal flower of ice.
The wide winter constellations
Set in fog brimming over
The seaward hills. Out beyond them,
In the endless dark, uncounted
Minute clots of light go by,
Billions of light years away,
Billions of universes,
Full of stars and their planets
With creatures on them swarming
Like all the living cells on the earth.
They have a number, and I hold
Their being and their number
In one suety speck of jelly
Inside my skull. I have seen them
Swimming in the midst of rushing
Infinite space, through a lens of glass
Through a lens of flesh, on a cup of nerves.
The question is not
Does being have meaning,
But does meaning have being.
What is happening?
All day I walk over ridges
And beside cascades and pools
Deep into the Spring hills.
Mushrooms come up in the same spot

In the abandoned clearing.
Trillium and adder's tongue
Are in place by the waterfall.

A heron lifts from a pool
As I come near, as it has done
For forty years, and flies off
Through the same gap in the trees.
The same rush and lift of flapping wings,
The same cry, how many
Generations of herons?
The same red tailed hawks court each other
High on the same rising air
Above a grassy steep. Squirrels leap
In the same oaks. Back at my cabin
In the twilight an owl on the same
Limb moans in his ancient language.
Billions and billions of worlds
Full of beings larger than dinosaurs
And smaller than viruses, each
In its place, the ecology
Of infinity.
I look at the rising Easter moon.
The flowering madrone gleams in the moonlight.
The bees in the cabin wall
Are awake. The night is full
Of flowers and perfume and honey.
I can see the bees in the moonlight
Flying to the hole under the window,
Glowing faintly like the flying universes.
What does it mean. This is not a question, but an exclamation.

KENNETH REXROTH'S
SIERRA PROSE

From An Autobiographical Novel (1964, expanded 1991)

From CHAPTER 30

After being around Seattle for a little and writing a couple of stories for *The Industrial Worker*, I decided to pull out. I hitchhiked up north, through Bellingham and Sedro Woolley, looking for work. I discovered nearby the largest white spot on the map, the largest spot without a road, that was not a desert, in the United States. I hitchhiked up the Skagit River to Marblemount, where, in those days, the road ended. From there on, around the headwaters of Lake Chelan and down to the Columbia River, was a roadless wilderness—the heart of the highest Cascades.

At Marblemount was a ranger station, where I got a job. Almost forty years later I was to meet Gary Snyder, who had worked for the same district ranger just before his retirement. At this time the ranger was just starting. He was what they call a local man in the Forest Service—he was not a forestry college graduate. His name was Tommy Thompson and he was a wonderful fellow. He eventually became Chief Ranger of the Baker National Forest.

I came in the evening with a rucksack on my back and asked for a job. He said, "Come on in and have supper. Maybe I've got a job." I didn't know anything about work in the woods.

They didn't have fire lookouts yet in that country. It was difficult to get stock through, and the Forest Service didn't have enough stock to go around, so this boy and I were sent out on different trails as patrolmen. I think the office of patrolman has practically disappeared from the Forest Service, and if it exists it's mounted, but we set out on foot to open up the country in the spring. He went

up the Skagit and up, I think, Richardson Creek, and I went up
Cascade Creek and over Cascade Pass and down in the Chelan Na-
tional Forest to Stehekin at the head of Lake Chelan and came back
over Agnes Glacier and down the Suiattle River to Marblemount
again. This was some of the wildest country in America and I had
never been in real mountains, except as a child sightseeing in the
Alps. Thompson gave me a short crosscut saw. I said, "Oh, are we
going together?" He said no. I said, "Who's going to pull the other
end of this? It hasn't got any handle on it." He said, "There isn't
going to be anybody to pull the other end of it. You'll do it alone."
Off I went with a rucksack on my back with a week's supply of food
and a couple of light tools and a crosscut saw and ax. The distance
was not great, but between Marblemount and Stehekin I did the
work which later would be assigned to a CCC crew of twelve boys.
I had no pack horse and nobody to give me any advice. I did what
seemed to need doing. I sawed open the trail. In one of our tool
caches I found some dynamite and an auger. At that cabin I camped
with an old hardrock miner who said I was wasting my energy. He
showed me a little of elementary powder-man technique. After that
I blew open the windfalls. I bored a hole in the log, put in a little
powder and a cap, and blew it to pieces. On the way back on the
other trail, which was extremely rough and steep—in those days
it was impossible to get stock over the Suiattle River trail—I blew
my way out of the country, but going in I sawed my way. There
were plenty of tool caches. You don't camp out in that country, it's
too wet, particularly on the Sound slope. All through the country
there were cabins to stay in where there were supposed to be tools
for Forest Service use. A saw and an ax would not keep very well
over the winter, so those two things I carried, but there were bars,
peevees, mauls, picks, hammers, wedges, and dynamite cached all
over the country. I tipped rocks into mudholes and pulled rocks
out of the rocky spots and leveled off the trail, and was a one-man

trail crew and thought nothing of it, because I'd never seen such things before. I got back probably the happiest boy who ever lived.

The trip took a little less than two weeks. I got another week's supply at Stehekin at the head of Lake Chelan for the return trip. My job was not actually to repair the trail going in but to open the country up after the winter so the trail crew with stock could get through behind me. In those two weeks or so I discovered the whole world of the Western mountains. I camped with Basque sheepherders, insane prospectors, and cattle outfits, and climbed all the most interesting peaks along the way in the early morning or in the evening after I was through work.

One weekend I was above Lake Chelan with Glacier Peak far off across the steep canyon to the west. It didn't look particularly near. I was not deluded by the distance, but I was deluded by the apparent ease of access. I started off Friday night down the canyon with no experience of the dense understory of the Puget Sound rain forest. In a short time I found myself hopelessly entangled in a jungle of down timber, vine maple, devil's club, and blackberry bushes, all growing on a surface at the steepest possible angle. Sometimes I would descend for a hundred feet scrambling in and out of branches like a monkey without ever touching ground. My shirt got torn and my knuckles barked, my eyes smarted with lashing branches. I kept on because after I had gone a little way it was impossible to get back up. I reached the river at the bottom of the canyon after about three hours. The climb up the other side, although steeper, was not so difficult and I got to the broad meadows on the western side of Glacier Peak the afternoon of the next day. It had taken me several hours to cover an airline distance of little over a mile.

I built a fire and made some tea and sat eating hardtack and cheese. All round me like a herd of domestic sheep were Rocky Mountain goats. As the sun set, just like domestic kids and lambs, the young ones played over the grass, up and down the hummocks and protruding rocks and down timber at follow-the-leader and king-of-the-mountain. To the southwest the great mountain rose up covered with walls of ice. There was no one near me for many miles in any direction. I realized then with complete certainty that this was the place for me. This was the kind of life I liked best. I resolved to live it as much as I could from then on. By and large I've kept that resolve and from that day much of my time and for some years most of my time was spent in the Western mountains.

When I got back to Marblemount I took a one-week trip up to the headwaters of Skagit River along the Canadian border in an even wilder and steeper country of sharp granite peaks. I tried to arrange my itinerary so that I'd have a peak to climb every evening after work. This was along the Richardson Creek–Fraser River watershed and official first ascents were not to be made in this country until ten to twenty years later. I knew nothing about such matters as mountaineering records and still less about mountaineering techniques and nothing about the unsportsmanlike evils of solo climbing. I scrambled up everything that looked difficult and steep and watched the sunset and came down. I suppose I could have been killed many times over because some of the peaks involved long passages as difficult as the climbs around Chamonix. I had never read about laybacks or kneeing up a crack. I just did it. I didn't have sense enough to know how dangerous it was. In fact, the only place where I ever feared for my life was the climb over the jackstraw tangle up and down the east wall of the Suiattle River on the way to Glacier Peak. When I got back to Marblemount the second time, I discovered I was bumped by a forestry student from the University of Washington.

From CHAPTER 39

We went off to the Sierras whenever we could, even if the main road
to Yosemite (this was before either tunnel) was closed. We hitch-
hiked up the steep, dirt Sand Hill Road. Once during that warm
California autumn we spent about a week in the Yosemite Valley.

There were big fish in the Merced River, some so big, in fact, that
two fish made a supper for us. Then against everybody's advice, we
hiked up to Tuolomne Meadows and over Mono Pass and down
Bloody Canyon, to the Valley and back to Lee Vining and Bridge-
port. We turned around and went back down to Bishop and around
the mountains, through the Mojave, and back up to San Francisco.
Of course there were no concrete highways, no highway over the
mountains. The east side of Tioga Pass Road was still a rough min-
ers' road. I don't believe there was a connection between Tuolumne
Meadows and the mining road down below. Anyway, we didn't go
down that way. Highway 395 was not what anybody would call a
highway in those days, and the whole country at that time of year
was deserted. It was quite wonderful to have camped in Tuolumne
Meadows in a warm late autumn with no one there at all. Then
a storm came up, and it began to snow as we went down Mono
Pass. I know now we had done something very foolish and danger-
ous. We debated climbing Mt. Lyell. Had we done so, we prob-
ably would have been mercilessly exterminated by the onset of the
weather. However, we did climb Mt. Gabb. That was not the first
of innumerable trips into the Sierras, but the one that I remember
best. It was Andrée's birthday when we were in Yosemite. We had
trout and a bannock birthday cake stuffed with black figs and nuts.

As winter came on, we began to read about immense snow-
falls in the Sierras. We could hardly believe our eyes. We decided
we had to go skiing there. We tried to find out something about

conditions, but we couldn't get any information at all.... We did find some skis, after a good deal of trouble, stored away at a sporting goods store.

There we met a skier who gave us some advice. But the best information we got came from Leo Eloesser, one of the first ski mountaineers. He was a famous surgeon, a world-famous doctor, and perhaps the most remarkable man in California.... Leo and a friend were the first people up Shasta on skis. He climbed all sorts of mountains hardly anybody knew existed in those days, like White Mountain. I think he climbed all the 14,000 peaks in California on skis. Both he and the man in the sporting goods store advised us to go to Cisco on the Donner Summit Road and then go north of the road just a short distance to a chain of lakes in a long valley parallel with the shoulder. There were in those days rather steep dirt roads built by the PG&E from one dam to another, and we would have open country, past Castle Rock Peak and around and down to Donner Lake and on to Truckee. Or we could go on north to the Feather River highway and railroad. There, Leo told us, was the best skiing in America....

Our snow equipment was very primitive, but we had a wonderful time making it. For those days, it was really good. Some of it we simply invented. Some we had information about, but that described equipment which was much too heavy. We did have sleeping bags, and Egyptian cotton covers for them—all of this waterproofed with alumina gel which we mixed and precipitated into the things ourselves, something I still prefer to complete waterproofing because it breathes. The great trouble with modern equipment is that it is impermeable....

Anyway, we toiled laboriously through the forest, following a trail that wasn't very steep. By our Eastern standards, for winter and all that snow, it was quite warm. We didn't know any turns except the Telemark, which is not for ordinary California snow. You've got to have pretty good powder snow to go Telemarking around with much success. So we developed something very much like modern skiing, that is, weighted parallel turns.... Coming down off the mountain to Donner Lake, we were quite frightened at the steepness of the slopes, but we managed to get down. Twice we stayed at inns which were closed for the winter, but the owners were living there. We spent about eight days, I think, skiing all around and camped on the snow for five nights. That was our first trip into the winter mountains, something that would be repeated again and again.

No matter the season, we were able to get away from the main trails, which was not a common thing to do in those days. One fall afternoon, we hiked down one of the old lumber roads from our camp near Hume Lake. Andrée had spent the morning painting, and I had been botanizing and writing. At the end of the road, we met a group of convicts who were living across the valley of Hume Creek. They were building a road that would eventually reach the floor of the Kings Canyon and go on to the upper basin, the valley which greatly resembles the Yosemite Valley, and which could only be reached then by trails over the top. In return for mailing their letters, the convicts showed us a trail that had been built up the floor of the canyon by the engineers who were surveying the road. It entered the upper basin through Cedar Grove, a dense wood of incense cedar at the other end. The convicts had concealed the trail with timber and brush, so no one else knew about it except a few of them who had gone up there for fishing. So we hiked up to the upper valley.

Because it was the fall, the water was way down and we could easily get back and forth across the river. Earlier in the year, the fords were impossible to navigate for a person on foot. For all intents and purposes, a great stretch of the Kings Canyon was open to us alone. We never saw anyone. Usually, we were below the snow line, that is, lower than Yosemite Valley. We could have stayed there until late in the year, at least until Thanksgiving.

Midway up the trail there was a cabin which had belonged to
a prospector, trapper, and general mountain rat by the name of Put
Boyden. He had discovered a cave at this point which later became
one of the sights to see in Kings Canyon National Park, kept closed
by huge iron gates so that people would not get lost in there, and to
prevent vandalism, the curse of national parks, national forests, and
city parks. Put Boyden's cabin was a little shingle hut, with a bunk
and a stove. In front was a broad deep pool in the river where the
current was still enough for swimming and full of immense fish, the
largest of which were almost as long as my lower leg. The smallest
fish weighed about a pound and a half. We only had to toss in a fly
to pull out a meal. That gave us a plentiful protein supply, and we
could carry in on our backs three weeks of dry food.

Not far above our camp, some timber fell across the river and
formed a logjam which made a bridge. So we could get all the way
to the upper valley in the spring of the year when the water was
too high to ford anywhere else. It was a little dangerous, but it was
worth it. The Kings River Valley in spring was an immense flower
garden, covered very thickly with tricolor lupines. In the meadows
and up in the shady sides was every imaginable flower of that eleva-
tion. We'd go in and stay a month. We made a huge herbarium
there. When our supplies ran short, I'd hike out, twelve miles or so,
to Hume to get some food and come back. No one was around yet
because there was still snow on the way over the bench from Lake
Hume. So we had our refuge all to ourselves. It's extraordinary to
think that then we could spend six weeks in California and never
see another human being.

Most travel was done with packhorses and mounted tourists.
There were few backpackers like us. We'd go off the trail wherever
the country was relatively level and travel with geological survey
topographical contour maps. So I began the habit of living under
the stars, later even in the winter. Until very recent years I've spent

most of the year living outdoors....

All of this had tremendous influence on us. My poetry and philosophy of life became what it's now fashionable to call ecological. I came to think of myself as a microcosm in a macrocosm, related to chipmunks and bears and pine trees and stars and nebulae and rocks and fossils, as part of an infinitely interrelated complex of being. This I have retained.

Remarkably, during our mountain travels, Andrée never had any epileptic attacks, which convinced her that her illness was psychogenic. (She eventually became disabused of this idea; it was obvious that it was not.) ... She never had even a *petit mal* in the water. Similarly with mountaineering. We eventually did a lot of rock climbing, some glacier climbing elsewhere, not in California, and ski mountaineering, and she never had any trouble. That first year in California was a period of intense activity....

When Andrée discovered the distant landscape of the mountains, and the near landscapes of trees, rocks, and waterfalls, she was entranced. She'd always take watercolors and paper along, even on winter trips, find a sheltered spot in the sun, and sit there and paint watercolors on top of eighteen feet of snow. I was writing and painting, and the creative outpouring never stopped.

From CHAPTER 51

... By this time Andrée and I had begun to live separately.... We made one more trip to the Sierras together and stayed in our hidden camp on the south fork of the Kings River until November.

The next year, Andree didn't want to go.... I returned from a long trip in much higher country than we had ever penetrated.

From CHAPTER 52

... I could go on for many pages with tales like this, but I have told these not just as jokes, but as an indication of an important aspect of Marie's character—a sense of humor both ironic and frisky. She attended the poetry class which I held in my own very large furnished room—something I have done practically all my life—but the first considerable time we spent together, living together so to speak, was on a long trip backpacking into the High Sierras. She was the nurse at a fashionable Jewish camp, "Singing Trail," at the Huntington Lake back of Fresno. When camp closed, I hitchhiked up, met her, and we started off for the high country for three weeks of backpacking.

My pack astonished her. It was so heavy that it was extremely difficult to lift off the ground onto my shoulders. I would put it on a stump or a downed timber, adjust the shoulder strap and the tumpline around my forehead. She would pull me to my feet, and we'd start off. We got a ride from the ranger up the narrow dirt road to Florence Lake and Blaney Meadows hot springs, and from there by easy stages to the pass below Mount Humphries (*sic*) above Desolation Basin. In those days, the High Sierra streams swarmed with trout, mostly golden trout, a subspecies of rainbow, once peculiar to one stream near Mt. Whitney, but since planted everywhere above eleven thousand feet. They're not the best eating, but catching them is like pulling out a living flame. So in a few minutes I could catch all the fish we could eat.

One day we climbed up to Desolation Lake and went swimming. Afterwards we lay on the granite sand and speculated on how difficult Mt. Humphries would be to climb. It certainly looked difficult. Suddenly I said, "Look, somebody's climbed it, there's somebody on the top. And there's something else there I can't quite make out." Finally we were able to tell what it was—a fox terrier.

So we decided the mountain could certainly be climbed and up we went. It was not easy. It is still considered one of the difficult west faces in the Sierras (the steep climbs are mostly on the east face of the Sierra fault block.). Near the summit we came on the High Sierra polemonium—dense clusters of deep blue flowers with the most beautiful floral odor I know. And just before we had passed through five hundred feet of almost equally beautiful Sierra primrose. In the twilight we passed through clouds of perfume. It was quite dark when we got back to the lake, and we picked our way off down the plateau in the moonlight, ate our supper of golden trout, risotto, and dried fruit, made love, and slept till the sun woke us up.

Every year after that we went to the mountains, eventually to cover the Sierras from Yosemite to Sequoia Park. We soon tired of trying to pack three weeks of supplies on our backs. And each year we rented a burro, usually in Sequoia Park if we were going into the southern Sierras, from there always the same burro, whom we called Bebe and who must have been as old as the rocks among which she shit, for she was marked by a running iron with the brand of the Kings River Packing Corporation, which dated back to the days of Jack London and Stewart Edward White. She was the wisest equine animal I have ever known. It was not necessary to tether or hobble her. She always stayed near camp, and in the evening would come and lie down near the fire like a dog.

We came to spend more and more time in high country at or above the timberline and off the trails. Sometimes we would go down with the donkey and load her up with wood and come back to the high lake. About the same time we began to climb with a rope—fourth- or fifth-class climbing—but without pitons. I have never liked mechanical aides in rock climbing—besides the nuisance of carrying all that hardware around. Snow goes from the summits of the Sierras in July, and the more difficult climbs are on very homogeneous granite, something like Chamonix in France. I have never cared much for climbing on ice and snow, although I've spent many hours cutting steps with an ice ax. I much prefer the acrobatics of difficult rock climbing. The Saw Tooth Range in northeastern Yosemite Park is granite with large crystals of plagioclase feldspar about the size of cubes of sugar. It provides, as it were, its own hobnails. Nevertheless, the traverse of The Three Teeth is nothing to sniff at. At one point you rope down to the end of your doubled rope about a hundred and fifty feet, drive in a heavy piton, attach a carabiner, and attach a rope sling to that, put your feet in the sling, pull down the rappel rope, thread it through the carabiner, wrap it around yourself, and throw yourself backwards into space.

We joined the rock climbing section of the Sierra Club and went on most of their weekend practice trips on local rocks, but never on one of the High Sierra trips. I have a strong distaste for group activities in the mountains. I can sympathize with the insane Englishman encountered by one of the Everest expeditions, who set off to climb the mountain alone and was never seen again. But I found a few friends who enjoyed winter camping, ski touring, and mountaineering, and made a complete outfit for the purpose—goose-down mummy bag, coffin-shaped tent which could be pitched to anything upright or in an X by two thick rubber bands cut from an inner tube, on crossed skies in front and ski poles behind. I used a high count, long staple, Egyptian cotton spinnaker cloth and dyed it the most brilliant red I could obtain.... My tent would hold just three men, very close together in their sleeping bags with their duffel at the long narrow end. I used it for many years in the blazing sun of spring skiing in the Sierra Nevada. It never faded. Then I loaned it to a friend who was going to the Himalayas. It came back the palest apricot color. Otherwise I still have it, and it's as good as ever—over forty years old.

Ski touring and mountaineering have given me some of the

happiest moments of my life. It's not just swinging long turns down
a steep mountainside, or traveling through the snow-bound forest
where the tree tops stick up like little Christmas trees, but even
crawling out at night to piss under the black sky full of billions
of stars shedding a pale grey light in the infinite expanse of snow.
One is tempted to write one's initials doing this, while realizing
under planets, stars, and nebulae, and surrounded by peaks heaved
up in the Jurassic, that like Keats "here lies one whose name was
writ in water."

As I look back on the period between the wars, with all its busy
work and endless meetings in the labor movement, mass strikes, po-
lice attacks and killings, and all the other seemingly eventful activi-
ties, what I remember clearly are stones and trees and flowers and
snow, and the companionship of my wife. "*Tout passé, ils demeurent.*"

From CHAPTER 53

Once Marie and I were hiking up the Kern River Canyon, headed
for Mt. Whitney and the Whitney Plateau. We stopped where
Golden Trout Creek crossed the trail. The fish were washing down
the creek, which was still in spate. I left Marie with the rucksacks
and a box of flies and climbed up the steep creek, jerking out trout
from over my head. When I had caught the limit, I came down.
Marie had taken a Royal Coachman fly on its leader and held it
over the ten-foot wide pool which had been created by the ford,
dangling the fly a few inches from her hand. She too had caught
the limit—the first trout she ever caught. "What on earth are we
going to do with all these fish?" I said.

Just then along the trail came two men walking with an im-
mense mule. We offered them half the fish, and when they saw the
size of our packs—mine weighed over a hundred pounds—they

insisted on putting them on the mule. Their names were Leo and
Leon; the mule's name was Mexico. We traveled with them for the
next five days, and with them climbed Mt. Whitney and several
other more difficult peaks. They wouldn't let us use our grub. As
is usually the case, they had taken far more than they needed. They
couldn't cook, so I did the cooking. They turned out to be Russian
emigrés.

... To Leon, the Bolshevik Party was essentially a police orga-
nization of double agents who were also working for various for-
eign governments. It was a weird experience struggling up narrow
couloirs to the top of fourteen-thousand-foot peaks and hearing
all this stuff from the other end of the rope. At the time, I put it
down to the bitterness of a disappointed man, but now I believe
most of it.

... Leon was a tall, thin man with a long face and what is called
a grey complexion. He showed the signs of a lifetime of prisons
and exile interrupted by short periods of terrorist activity. He was
continuously driven. He always hiked on ahead, faster than the
rest of us, and couldn't get enough mountains to climb. Leo was a
stocky, black-haired ivory-skinned man who probably had Tatar or
Kalmukh blood. He was imperturbable. His only vice was Upman
cigars, which he smoked every night in camp and which the mule
carried in a special humidor.

From CHAPTER 60

Due to the rationing of gasoline, it was difficult to go to the Sierras,
but all our free time was spent in the cabin in Devil's Gulch in the
northern corner of Marin County, now Samuel Taylor State Park.
Twice we took our vacations there, and often when I was there
alone I would devote much of my time to systematic meditation....

I look back with nostalgia and awe at the nights I spent alone in the little cabin in Devil's Gulch, sitting in the lotus posture, doing controlled breathing, and emptying my mind of its detritus. There was nothing but the firelight and the sound of the two waterfalls that came down and joined directly under the cabin. I had a pet kingsnake who used to like to lie inside my shirt, and although you can't make a pet of an owl unless you feed him live mice, the same owl came every night to sit on a shattered tree in front of the cabin and sing to me. There is a sign on the map of Samuel Taylor State Park headquarters, "This way to the Rexroth cabin," but eventually I was not allowed to use it. Now the steep gully has washed out the trail, and the cabin itself has collapsed. Maybe someday it will be rebuilt, for there I wrote most of the poems in *The Phoenix and the Turtle* and others in *The Signature of All Things*.

From CHAPTER 61

When the war ended, our lives changed drastically... Life opened up for us. Gasoline was no longer rationed, and we could travel and go to the Sierras both summer and winter. The psychological pressure of a world at war and the physically exhausting work were both gone. I wrote a great deal more poetry, and about this time wrote the series of plays in the book *Beyond the Mountains*.

The first years, then, after World War II were full of happiness, donkey trips in the High Sierras that lasted all summer, the parties, meetings, and poetry readings of the Libertarian Circle. More important were the spaghetti and steak, wine and music parties at home with our more intimate friends, usually only four couples.

From Camping in the Western Mountains
(1939, published online 2002)

From Chapter One, "Minimum Equipment"

The first thing anybody does when planning a camping trip is to
make a list, and probably that is as good a way as any to start a book.
This is a list of the essential equipment for two knapsackers for two
weeks. It is, as it were, succinct and to the point; there is nothing
in it that can conveniently be done without. It will provide a sort
of base from which to work, an irreducible minimum to which
we can add as we go along. Once in a while one encounters those
strange legendary creatures who live on rice and fish, sleep in their
clothes and a pieces of canvas, and who are content with a fishing
line, a few flies, a jackknife, a coffee can and some matches. They
would despise such a conglomeration of stuff, but fortunately they
have passed far beyond the reach of camping manuals. Others, who
in the past have emerged from sporting goods stores staggering
under a "complete equipment" suggested by some salesman's fertile
brain, will be struck with horror.

Clothing for each person:

>   waterproofed boots
>   two pairs of heavy wool boot socks
>   waist overalls
>   two blue chambray shirts
>   suspenders or belt
>   slipover sweater
>   three bandana handkerchiefs
>   broadbrimmed hat

long wool underwear (for pajamas)
poncho
extra leather shoe laces
light broadcloth trunks

Optional clothing for each person:

basketball shoes
gloves
swim suits
dark glasses
mosquito veil
another sweater
cotton work socks
felt and cork insoles
light wool or silk gauze undershirt

Miscellaneous equipment:

jackknife (Boy Scout type)
"pocket" axe or machete or corn knife
can opener
small triangle file
sewing kit:
    needles
    linen thread
    darning wool
    pins
    safety pins
    "bachelor buttons" wrapped in a piece of denim
        for patching
    scissors

toilet kit:

>   soap
>
>   towels
>
>   razor and blades
>
>   toothbrushes
>
>   tooth powder
>
>   nail file

first aid kit:

>   1 oz. iodine (half-strength Lugol's solution)
>
>   roll of 3-inch bandage
>
>   roll of 2-inch adhesive tape
>
>   safety pins, wrapped in a sware yard of sterile muslin
>   and then in oiled silk
>
>   aspirin
>
>   cascara pills
>
>   4 oz. cod liver oil

metal mirror

flashlight, extra bulbs and batteries

writing kit:

>   pencils
>
>   paper
>
>   envelopes
>
>   post cards
>
>   stamps

fishing tackle:

>   rod
>
>   reel
>
>   leaders
>
>   line
>
>   flies
>
>   hooks

USGS maps

25 feet of cord
oiled silk and cloth bags for grub
boot grease
3 plumbers candles
waterproof match box
matches
tobacco in oiled silk pouch
compass watch
laundry soap
sleeping bags
packs
tent
cook kit:
    three nesting pots
    frying pan
    aluminum pans for dishes
    forks and spoons

There are two ways of being miserable in the mountains. First, you can go with too little equipment, shiver under inadequate bedding with a fire going all night, eat with your fingers out of the cooking pots, cower under a tree or walk all day soaked with rain, and come home in rags. On the other hand, you can let your imagination run riot in a large outfitting store, weight yourself down with all manner of contraptions and unnecessary clothing, most of which you will probably lose or discard, carry a tent which is too large to pitch on uneven ground and tips over or blows down in the night, sleep beneath twenty pounds of blankets and quilts, and stagger along the trail overladen and gasping. Quite a few ingenious souls manage to combine both methods. Either is guaranteed to bring you home exhausted and ten or more pounds underweight.

From CHAPTER FOUR, "THE CAMP"

A list is a fine thing, and just as equipment and provisions were
first reduced to simple lists and then expanded with comment, the
routine of camping itself can also be summarized. To the inexpe-
rienced, the following suggestions may seem altogether too much
of a routine, almost a drill. After all, camping is a sport. One goes
to the mountains to escape routine, to forget for a while the ef-
ficient monotony of earning a livelihood, to relax the tensions and
inhibitions of the struggle for existence, to loaf. Precisely for this
reason an order, an economy, of camp making is necessary, unless
one wishes to spend most of the time housekeeping. Puttering
around can be done just as well at home, there is not much sense
in traveling thirty miles from a road, climbing passes and fording
creeks, just to get in one's own way. And unless properly organized,
housekeeping, or rather campkeeping, will certainly monopolize
many precious hours.

   Pick your companions carefully, be sure they can adjust them-
selves to coordinated group work; examine yourself, be sure you
can and do. Nothing will spoil a trip more effectively than some-
one who bickers and shirks his responsibilities. Then divide up the
work, either permanently or in regular rotation. Have a packer and
horse wrangler, a cook, a dishwasher, someone responsible for the
tents and bedding, someone for wood and water. Be sure the work
is equally divided, then stick to the divisions. The ideal camp is a
miniature anarchist community, straight out of Kropotkin. Each
goes about his appointed task quietly and efficiently, the functions
of the group are shared with spontaneous equality, problems are
settled by consultation rather than controversy, and whatever lead-
ership exists is based solely on experience and ability. The moun-
tains and glaciers, the forests and streams of America are a heritage
shared equally by all the people, and they are not simply "recreation

areas," but training grounds for group living and group sharing. Each group that hikes or rides along the trail by day contented and alert, and makes camp at night "decently and in order" is a sort of test tube or kindergarten of the good life. So don't forget, when it's your turn to wash the dishes, the centuries are watching you.

CAMP ROUTINE, SMALL PARTIES, SHIFTING CAMP

Making Camp:

unpack
water and pasture or picket stock
inspect pasture fences and gates
stow harness
sling pulleys
pitch and ditch tent if stormy, dig hip hole
lay bed before ground gets damp
build or repair cooking fireplace
build or repair campfire place
dig latrine
gather and cut wood for supper and breakfast
cover wood if stormy
lay fires
get grub and utensils ready
bathe
fetch water for cooking and night
light cook fire
cook (keep grub and gear together)
eat
wash dishes
stow grub and gear on pulleys or under covers
light campfire

move picketed stock
take a look about
retire

Breaking Camp:

move and water picketed stock
bathe
fetch water
spread bed and break tents
light fire
cook, eat
wash dishes
pack, roll bed last
fetch and pack stock
burn refuse
cover latrine
take a last look
extinguish fires thoroughly
take another last look.

Excellent campsites are plentiful in the Sierra Nevada and seldom
more than four miles apart, usually much closer together. Until late
summer most of them have sufficient feed for one animal nearby;
large parties with several pack animals should inquire about feed
conditions from rangers and packers before starting and plan their
stops accordingly. USGS and Forest Service maps show all principal
meadows. Three generations of campers have equipped most of the
better campsites with tables, benches, bough beds, and fireplaces of
a more or less makeshift sort, and recently the Civilian Conservation
Corps has constructed a number of solidly built fireplaces and tables,
and sometimes latrines and refuse pits, in the more popular areas.

It is wisest to use these conveniences where they exist, camping at random along the trail litters the forest and increases the risk of fire.

With or without previously built conveniences, a good campsite should possess the following qualifications: (1) water; (2) wood; (3) drainage: (4) feed for stock; (5) a pool or lake for bathing; (6) an impressive view; (7) freedom from fire hazard; (8) a level spot for the beds, and trees or poles for the tent; (9) a fireplace or rocks to make one; and (10) privacy from other campers.

Firewood is abundant except on the desert ranges. It isn't of the very finest quality, no western tree can compare with shagbark hickory for cooking purposes, but most of it ignites easily and burns with a fat, hot flame, and due to the aridity of the climate and the well-drained soil, it is usually dry. Pine wood burns with a very sooty flame, and that is why an aluminum tray makes the best stove top. Use only dead wood; green coniferous wood, if it can be ignited at all, soon chars and goes out. In rainy weather squaw wood, that is, the lower dead branches of living trees, should be used to start fires. Don't disdain the high driftwood left along creeks by the spring floods. If dry it makes excellent firewood. Thick branches of dead brush are good too, in fact manzanita is probably California's best firewood. Most brush is so twisted that it balks beneath the axe and should be chopped with great care. Here is a list of the commonest woods and their fire-making qualities:

Sooty Woods:
All pines, timberline trees particularly

Less Sooty (in order of cleanness of flame):
dogwood
aspen
cottonwood

maple
buckeye
alder
cherry
manzanita
big tree
fir
cedar
spruce
Douglas fir

Hot Coals (in order):
manzanita
timberline wood
mountain mahogany
dogwood
maple
oak
wild plum
cedar (hot but brief)
limber pine (hot but brief)
big tree (hot but brief)
ceanothus
cherry

Quick Fires and Kindling (in order):
decayed timberline logs
lodgepole pine (particularly squaw wood)
very dry driftwood
dead manzanita
dry ceanothus and other chaparral
yellow pine

sugar pine
big tree, if very dry
cedar, if very dry
spruce
Douglas fir
fir
alder

Long Burning:
maple
cherry
ash
dogwood
cottonwood
alder
timberline trees, particularly juniper

As a general rule, the heavier the wood (if it is dry), the more
slowly it will burn; the harder the wood, the hotter the coals; the
softer the wood, if it be without pitch, the cleaner the flame. Woods
rich in pitch will give a fat, quick flame and a bright light. Rotten
wood, in the damp, deciduous forest of the East, is poor firewood;
it burns slowly, if at all, and makes a punky, smoky fire. Decayed
coniferous wood, on the other hand, particularly the firm outer
crust of decayed "short-haired" pine logs, makes a fine fire, and the
undersides of such logs, if they are clear of the ground, will provide
firewood in rainy weather. A small fire, just big enough to do the
work required of it, is best. Never build "bonfires" and never build
a fire against a tree, log, or stump.

If you had an unlimited supply of paper, matches, and time,
you could afford to build fires any which way, but since you are not
so supplied, it pays to learn how to do it properly. The most difficult

fire to build is one in rainy weather. I will describe that and you can
simplify the procedure to suit yourself.

Gather an armful of dry branches about as thick, at the butts,
as your thumb, from standing timber, another armful of similar
branches about two inches to three in diameter and an armful of
dry wood chopped from the center or underside of a decayed log.
Strip the bark from the branches and split them into four pieces.
Take four of the smallest pieces and shave them with your knife,
leaving the shavings attached to the stick. Make a little tent of these
towards the front of the fireplace with the curls down. If it is raining,
shelter them with your hat. Have the rest of the wood piled within
reach. Light the shavings, and as the flame catches, add the smallest
sticks first, one at a time, adjusting them to the flame and carefully
preserving the structure of the tent. Don't put on too much, give the
fire just enough to feed it as it grows. As soon as all the small sticks
have caught, add the large ones, crossing them carefully to leave
spaces between and beneath them for draught. If you wish to be very
precise, you can start the fire in a triangle of medium-sized sticks,
each laid with one end on the ground and one end on its neighbor,
and add the larger fuel, interlaced in similar fashion, to this base. If
you are an inexperienced camper, it is a good idea to build all fires
this way, then when you have to you will know how. Take care of
your matches, it is practically impossible to strike a hot spark from
granite, and a friction-stick fire requires exactly the right wood and
lots of experience.

Things are easily lost if strewn haphazardly around camp. Keep
everything you are not using packed away, and before dark lay out
all the food and utensils for supper with a flashlight on a poncho
near the fireplace.... Don't lay the cooking fork or knife on the
fireplace, it is liable to be knocked into the fire, or get hot and burn
your fingers. Some camp cooks seem to suffer from an occupational
neurosis, they work in a mounting fever of anxiety, verging on
hysteria. Keep calm and the supper will taste better.

Mountain trails are dusty and one perspires lavishly in the dry air. It is wise to bathe thoroughly at night and take a short dip every morning. Of course the water is cold, and it is painful at first for some, but it pays to persist, nothing is more refreshing, and if you don't, you will soon feel muggy and depressed and begin to itch.

Always wash the dishes immediately after eating; the longer you put it off, the more distasteful it becomes, and the harder the dishes are to get clean.

All wild animals are at least inquisitive about your supplies, and bears, wolverines, deer, rats, and even mice, can do sufficient damage to end the trip right there. Stow everything out of reach before you settle down around the campfire for the night. If you are careless, you may spend several nights without anything being harmed, but the fateful night is sure to come, and then it is too late.

From CHAPTER 6, "HORSES, MULES, BURROS, RIDING, PACK-ING, AND HORSE FURNITURE"

BURROS

Some packers and punchers who affect a Buffalo Bill sophistication without knowing much about their business, malign and belittle the burro. They insist he is stubborn, lazy and prone to kick and bite. What happens is that such men treat the little animal badly, overload him, feed him poorly and kick him around generally. He, with the wisdom of Egypt and the Ancient East from which he comes, stoically accepts his fate, bides his time, and when he gets a chance, returns an eye for an eye and a tooth for a tooth. This alone shows that he is a lot smarter than a horse, who can be hammered by a sadist into neurotic subjection. If you go camping every summer and have a place to keep him over the year, buy a young burro and break him in yourself. If you treat him properly

he will be as devoted and intelligent a pet and servant as any dog.
In the winter the children can ride him, or you can yourself if you
weigh 150 pounds or less and don't overdo it; and in the summer
he will carry 75 to 120 pounds up and down steep trails without
a murmur. A good burro, not spoiled by bad handling or too old,
will get along as fast as you care to walk, but not as fast as a large
spry horse. Carrying 75 pounds or less he can make his way over
any kind of terrain, short of actual mountain climbing. He will
stay in the meadow where you put him and not stray, in fact, if you
give him a little barley, salt, sugar or a bit of bread every day, his
principal fault will be a tendency to tag around after you like a dog.
He can be taught to go ahead of you and stop, if he meets a sign or
crosstrail, while you botanize in the hedgerows. He soon learns to
sound snow and keep away from pockets and bridges when cross-
ing a pass. He can estimate distances better than a mule, let alone
a horse, and seldom gets himself wedged in rocks. Loaded down,
he will navigate streams that would sweep you away. (I once almost
lost my life by following a burro into a high ford which he crossed
with ease.) He is a companionable beast, and if you let him, he likes
to come in and lie down near the edge of the firelight at night. If
you are traveling alone, this is welcome company, but I wouldn't
advise you to carry on long conversations with him; passing rang-
ers may get the impression that you are a little dotty. I never heard
of a house-broken horse, but a burro can be trained to respect the
precincts of a camp. He doesn't have to be shod, he can be trusted
to keep away from poison feed, he seldom gets sick, but usually dies
of old age, sometime after his thirtieth year, and he flourishes at
14,000 feet. In general, if he could only cook and pack himself, he
would be a lot better trail companion than many humans.

. . . I guess that is all about burros. I hate to leave the subject, it
is filled with pleasant memories. I hear the little animals are being
improved on. Perhaps you have heard of the llama, a docile, wide-

eyed creature rather like a small giraffe in woolen pajamas. They
were domesticated by the ancient Incas and have been used ever
since as beasts of burden in the high Andes. Someone in southern
California has started importing them and crossing them with bur-
ros. The resulting hybrid, called a burma if a male, and a llaro if a
female, is reputed to far surpass either parent in intelligence, agility
and durability; and as an added inducement, the oil of its wool, if
rubbed on the body, is excellent for dandruff, hot and cold flashes,
and aching feet. Probably the mountains of California soon will be
full of them. As yet they can be obtained only with difficulty and at
practically prohibitive prices.

SICKNESS

Horses suffer from a wide variety of sicknesses and injure themselves
in all sorts of ways. If the animal is seriously ill, let it alone, and go
for a ranger or at least a packer or puncher. Don't tamper with it
yourself. The three commonest ailments are wind colic, spasmodic
colic, and distemper. The first two are due to indigestion, caused by
drinking while too hot, overeating, or feed which the animal is not
used to. The animal may lie down frequently, roll, wander about
restlessly, belch, break wind and walk with its shoulders humped up
and put its feet down tenderly. If these symptoms are mild, there is
nothing to be distressed about, recovery is usually prompt. But if
he grunts and rolls violently, breaks into perspiration and quivers
with spasms, he has spasmodic colic, and is seriously ill. Go for help.

... If the physic has no effect, the animal's rectum may be
impacted. A handful of tobacco inserted in the anus will sometimes
cause the horse to expel the obstruction, or it can usually be re-
moved by hand. The hand and arm should be heavily coated with
grease and the horse tied to keep him from kicking. However in-
teresting this is as reading matter, it is wiser to leave the beast alone.

From CHAPTER NINE, "THE TRAIL"

THE TRAIL

The trail is what counts. Camp is very well, but too much time is occupied with housekeeping; the daily objectives, peaks, meadows, lakes, beautiful campsites, have the final, brief pleasure of achievement; but nothing can compare with the wonderful sense of freedom, the constantly varied interest, of travel through mountainous country.... The mountain landscape is infinitely varied and constantly changing. Movement is free, easy, relaxed; the streams are full of fish, the trees are full of birds, flowers grow by the trail, deer jump from their coverts, even the air is intoxicating. It is the fact that we are on our way that is important, where we are going is a minor detail.

In a sense the trail is the final subject of all this book. I have attempted to cover the problems of camp life briefly, but in sufficient detail to leave the actual hiking or riding free from the worst worries and discomforts. Beginning this chapter, I hope it will be short. I, for one, want no one else's words in my head when I am traveling through the mountains. During the rest of the year we get plenty of advice and admonition in the offices and factories in which we work.

Camping and mountaineering are a compensation for the inadequacies and restrictions of modern life, but they should be a relaxing compensation.... Take it easy. Maybe you won't go as far as you planned, maybe there will be peaks you will have to leave unclimbed, lakes you will have to visit some other time, but you will enjoy yourself. On the other hand, don't loaf. Travel a little every day, or if you lay over, busy yourself exploring the country, fishing or climbing. If you only make five miles the first day, that is all right. Lengthen your journey every day, at the end of two weeks you will be covering fourteen or more miles a day with ease.

■

KEEPING THE TRAIL

If the trail seems hopelessly lost and the country is not otherwise
impassable, it is best to rely on the topographical sheet and proceed
very carefully in the approximate direction. The trail will usually
turn up again after a few minutes. If the route is at all steep, rocky,
or dangerous the animals should be led, and if it is particularly so
the only thing to do is to let them stand and hunt for the trail until
you find it.

Most of the mountainous country west of the Continental
Divide is fairly open, and its contours and drainage are well defined.
Obtain the USGS topographical sheets for the region you plan to
traverse and study them carefully. Locate the principal landmarks,
high peaks, domes, etc., and form in your mind a picture of the
drainage and the elevation and direction of the ridges. Keep the
map in your hip pocket, and as you go along, locate yourself on it
occasionally. Take a look back every now and then so that you can
recognize the trail if you approach it from the opposite direction.
Continuous map reading soon becomes a habit, in fact almost a
vice; maps are usually brought back from a long trip worn to shreds;
but it is one habit whose overindulgence is beneficial. If you know
where you have gone every mile of the way, you are not likely to
get lost. Careful use of the map is of course essential if you travel
off the trail.

Some of the lateral ridges of the Sierra Nevada, particularly the
Silliman Crest on the northern boundary of Sequoia National Park,
form natural approaches of the most spectacular beauty to the main
crest. Intelligent map reading and use of the compass and a little
rock work now and then should enable an experienced knapsack
party to negotiate such routes with little trouble. Other similar
regions in the Sierra are the section of the main crest between

Evolution Valley and the headwaters of Mono Creek, the Monarch
Divide, various routes in the vicinity of Mt. Goddard, the Brewer
range and the Sphinx Crest, and the route from Brewer to Tyndall
near that purportedly was followed by Clarence King. Only on a
trip like this, away from other tourists and campers, does one realize
to the full the loneliness and sterile magnificence that constitute the
greatest appeal of the Sierra Nevada.

Such knapsack routes are not for amateurs, and should never
be attempted on one's first season in the mountains. If you are new
to the country, the main trails will seem wild and rugged enough.

From CHAPTER TEN, "CLIMBING"

CLIMBING

No book can teach mountaineering, and any decent discussion of
the subject would occupy more space than this book. If you are
completely inexperienced, or even if you are an amateur, find out
from the mountaineering club in your state those mountains on
your route which can be climbed by any tyro, and stick to them.
Of course the thrill of climbing consists in taking chances, but
only reasonable chances. If you are in doubt, go back. And don't
go places you can't get back from. Climbing down is often more
difficult than climbing up.

This section on climbing has caused me some worry, originally
there was a lot more of it. Mountaineering is a lot of fun and it
is a lot of fun to write about. Some poets still claim the privilege
of writing solely to please themselves, but this book can hardly be
considered art for art's sake, I have tried to keep before me the uses
to which it is likely to be put. Purely as a matter of literary form one

might expect a lot about mountaineering in a book on camping in
the mountains. After much cogitation I have drastically reduced this
section and left only a few words of warning and advice. You can't
climb mountains with a book in your hand, searching for serac,
couloir, or arête in the index when those entities present them-
selves, but the Lord knows, somebody might try it. It is better for
all concerned that such a contingency be eliminated beforehand.

From CHAPTER 12, "WINTER CAMPING"

Winter camping is a strenuous and exacting sport, even in the level
forests of the eastern United States and Canada. In the mountains
of the West it is, in addition, as dangerous as you care to make it.
However, the compensations are very great. Few of us will ever get
the opportunity to explore the Polar regions, but most of us have
been thrilled by the narratives of the great expeditions. Much of the
fascination of mountain landscape lies in its inhuman immaculate
grandeur. The story of the conquest of a great peak, Whymper's
long struggle with the Matterhorn, for instance, is like a Sopho-
clean tragedy; at the end of the story, at the summit, nothing has
happened to the peak, it is still there, unchanged and aloof, like the
destiny of the tragedians, but something momentous has happened
to the men.

Today unexplored lands, trackless forests and unclimbed peaks
are few and far away, but winter is a great obliterator of the signs
of man. Once the tracked area about the ski lodge is left behind,
and our skis are the first to cut the snow, we too can capture some-
thing of the wonder of the trails and bivouacs of Franklin, Saussure,
Nansen and Whymper. Even a short trip through high mountain
country, however well known the summer trail, is thrilling over
untracked snow.

Then too, the exploration and mapping of good ski routes through the mountains of the West is still in its earliest infancy. In this specialized sense, parties with an adequate amount of skill can really "open up the country" and perform very real service.

From The WPA Guide to California (1939)

Sequoia and General Grant National Parks cover the wildest country on the western slopes of the Sierra Nevada. Sequoia stretches from the headwaters of the Kings River on the north to the headwaters of the Tule River on the south. The tallest peaks of the High Sierra— barely dominated by Mount Whitney (14,495 alt.), highest point in the 48 states—bound it on the east and the foothills of the Sierra on the west. Bisecting the park from north to south is a jagged granite ridge, the Great Western Divide. West of the divide are the park's major accommodations and most popular attractions, its motor roads, and shorter trails. Here, in the 4,000- to 8,000-feet elevations, are the groves and forests of California big trees (*Sequoia gigantea*) for which Sequoia is best known. Paralleling the divide for 25 miles, about halfway between it and the crest of the Sierra, are the 3,000-foot walls of the Kern River Canyon. In the eastern section of Sequoia are high mountain lakes—of glacial origin, as are the mountainsides of exposed rock and the great, irregular granite ridges, cleared of their earth and vegetation by ice thousands of years ago....

When Hale D. Tharp, a farmer from Three Rivers, visited Sequoia in 1856 in search of pastures and a ranch site, he was met by peaceful Yokut. "The Indians liked me," Tharp said later, "because I was good to them. I liked the Indians too, for they were honest and kind to each other. I never knew of a theft or murder among them." In 1858 Tharp discovered Giant Forest and first saw the big trees, one of which already had been described to him by the Indians as being so large that it took 25 men, with hands clasped together, to encircle it.

The settlers who followed Tharp to the Three Rivers region

were less popular with the Yokut; by 1862 their increasing num-
bers were forcing the Indians to retreat into the canyons of the
lower ranges. At this time they contracted their first white man's
diseases—smallpox, measles, and scarlet fever—and perished by
the hundreds, crawling, unless restrained by force, into their sweat
houses to die. Very simply, one of their leaders, Chief Chappo, had
Tharp ask the white men to go away. When told by his friend that
the settlers refused to leave, Tharp said that the chief and his braves
"sat down and cried." By 1865 the last of the tribe had retreated
into the mountains.

From "Yosemite National Park"

Yosemite Valley is a U-shaped trough, 7 miles long with an aver-
age width of one mile, sunk 3,000 feet below the rim of the park
and carved out of the granite slab of the Sierra by stream erosion
and massive glacial action. The floor is level and parklike, with
the Merced River meandering through its meadows and forests,
dominated by immense domes and rock masses, which form a sheer
wall around it. Dr. Bunnell, the man who named Yosemite, was so
moved by the valley that he wrote years afterward, "As I looked at
the grandeur of the scene a peculiar exalted sensation seemed to
fill my whole being, and I found my eyes in tears with emotion."

From Rexroth's newspaper columns
in the *San Francisco Examiner*

AUGUST 7, 1960

For the next couple of weeks we are going on a pack trip in the
southern Sierra. Nothing startling. We don't intend to make fires
by striking two photographers together, sleep in trees, or dine on
muddy dandelions. Just a square type outing.

We will go to Mineral King, above Visalia on the edge of
Sequoia National Park, and ride over the hump and have the man
leave us with a couple of donkeys. From there on we'll travel or
"set" as we please. If we don't want to pack up the donkeys and
travel, the children can ride them around the meadows. It's the
finest part of the Sierra, the high plateau and peak country just
west of Mt. Whitney. If you get off the main trails, as you can with
donkeys, it is still pretty unspoiled.

I know plenty of places where there are beautiful lonely lakes,
lots of fish, good feed for the donkeys, and few or no people pass-
ing by all summer. There are all kinds of peaks to climb if we want
to climb them, some you can ride a horse up, others amongst the
trickiest in the country.

... For going on 30 years I have spent most of my summers
this way. Last year we were in Europe, the year before in the Gros
Ventres Mountains in the Wyoming Rockies. I'll be glad to get
back. I have always felt I was most myself in the mountains. There
I have done the bulk of what is called my creative work. At least it
is in the mountains that I write most of my poetry.

Life in the city in the winter seems too full of distractions and
busy work. Who said poetry was emotion recollected in tranquil-
ity? I don't know about others, but I find most tranquility camped

by a mountain lake at timber line. There whatever past emotion and experience I choose to recollect and write down, take on most depth and meaning.

... Most men are like that fellow Hercules wrestled with, Antaeus. If they can make contact with the earth every once in a while, they keep their strength. Of course, a lot of people don't know this, and so they wonder what's wrong with them.

AUGUST 14, 1960

Well, we all came back from our pack trip unscathed and fit as fiddles. We decided to go deluxe and ride every day instead of being packed in and left with a couple of donkeys. This, of course, delighted our little girls, and as for father, there's nothing like 20 or more miles a day on horseback over mountain trails to jar off the grease....

It's a wonderful way to capture just a little of the feeling of the Old West. In fact, I guess it's the only way left. When I was a boy, bumming around the West out of Chicago, I bought myself a little zebra dun up in Horse Heaven Country in central Washington. I rode him all over the intermountain country, drifting from job to job—just like Hashknife Hartley, the Cowboy Detective, or one of Ernest Haycock's heroes. Each fall I'd board him out where I happened to be, and next spring I'd come back and get him.

I, too, have ambled down off the rimrock to the green homestead in the box canyon, building a wheatstraw "cigareet" with one hand while the sun set over the distant mountains. To my children this will be as improbable as though I claimed to have fought at Waterloo or Thermopylae.

How little time ago, and it's all gone. Still, you can imagine it back, riding down the switchbacks of Black Rock Pass, the

Kaweahs rising in front of you and a lightning storm battering the pinnacles. I can, anyway, and whatever my daughters imagined, they so obviously just loved it.

Nights under the thick stars, dawn swims in the cool mirror of a lonely lake, golden trout that quarrel to climb on your fly, vast stretches of park-like forest where nobody ever comes, meadows like square mile bowling greens full of elderly bucks with top heavy antlers—they are still there. Some day I'll be too old, but I will still have some wonderful memories to wander in.

JULY 2, 1961

Big doings in Tuolomne Meadows in Yosemite Park, with the dedication of the finally complete new Tioga Pass Road. Plenty of ceremony and celebration and celebrities, but everybody was a little embarrassed. You could smell the twinges of conscience in the air.

Only recently an outstanding spokesman for the Department of the Interior had referred to the project as a serious mistake. Here was a case where recreation and conservation had collided and, in the opinion of the authorities, conservation had been pushed aside, if not totally wrecked.

Is this true? I am by way of being a rabid conservationist myself, but I wonder. What is conservation for? In the final analysis it is always for people. Unless we are sentimentalists, we don't conserve the bison or the Big Trees for themselves, but for us.

... As the population explosion goes on exploding and our environment grows more and more mechanical and man-made we must be ceaselessly vigilant to defend and preserve those remnants of the environment from which we came, the organic web of life that nurtured our ancestors when they first started chipping rocks. However we as a species come to crowd the earth, let's hope we can always save enough of the pre-human world so that we can at least imagine ourselves as part of the balance of Nature. If we don't, as the fellow said, I don't know what will happen to us.

Reverence for life in the abstract is fine, but I am willing to let Albert Schweitzer worry about the spirochetes his injections kill. My reverence is for human life. So I am all for the preservation of wilderness areas, but not just so the bears can look at each other.

Conservation does not mean locking up sections of the natural environment in museum vaults from which the public is effectively excluded. It means careful, intelligent use that disrupts the non-human ecology as little as possible.

Careful, reverent use comes from the attitude of a whole people, not from a table of prohibitions thought up by the authorities. Switzerland is a pretty crowded country, and yet a lot of it looks pretty much as it did to Hannibal. England is still more densely and far more uniformly populated. No people has ever had a greater love for their countryside. True, it doesn't look much like it did to Julius Caesar, it looks much prettier.

The point of all this is that while I am prepared to resist any attempt to build a road over the Sierra through the Kings River Canyon or to turn the Golden Gate Park Panhandle into parking lots, I don't see any great virtue in refusing to improve an existing road that the public insists on using anyway. After all, the public have a right to at least one place in the state where they can drive to high mountain meadows and Alpine lakes. In this instance they have been voting for the right with 40 years of boiling engines and burnt out bearings.

The real conservation problems in Yosemite are, first, the rescuing of the Valley itself from imminent destruction, and second, the education of the public.

I believe all overnight use of the floor of Yosemite Valley should be abolished within the next 20 years. Perhaps the hotel and a few camps could stay for the use of conventions and conferences and other public activities, something like Asilomar. As it is, the place is an outdoor slum.

On the second point, trails, camps and viewpoints littered with gum and film wrappers and beer cans are far more dangerous than the paving and widening of a few miles of mountain road. Switzerland and England are beautiful because of the taste and sensibility of their people. A nation that doesn't give a damn how much of a mess it makes wherever it goes can pass all the laws and create all the primitive areas and national parks it wants, but it won't begin to understand the meaning of conservation.

Believe me, this is not just the good old editorial about litterbugs. What we call conservation comes out of a kind of spiritual courtesy. It is a Confucian virtue. Confucius had a word for it, he called it "human heartedness."

JULY 12, 1961

With my two daughters I've been visiting the High Sierra Camps run by the Curry Company in Yosemite. I want to do a travel piece on them—they are the ideal introduction to the mountains—but first I want to say a bit about their significance for what I feel must be a new philosophy of conservation.

They are an almost perfect example of controlled use of one of most important human resources—the still intact American wilderness.

We are still blessed in this country with a vast reservoir of undistorted, genuinely unspoiled, wild country where mankind has so far interfered with nature very little, if at all. This is not just a "wildlife resource," it is a human resource, a reservoir of recreation, peace and contemplation.

Use which preserves these values is conservation. Use which destroys or inhibits them is not.

The days of the old style Wild West use of the mountains are gone. Time was when a party of professional people of moderate means thought nothing of hitting the Sierra trails with 30 head of pack and saddle horses and an assortment of packers and cooks and guides.

Everybody got drunk, the fish weighed two pounds each and fought for the privilege of swallowing hooks, deer came to rock salt discreetly planted by the guides during the summer and asked to be shot, and all season long the horses gobbled up the meadows while the tin cans grew alongside camp.

For better or worse this sort of thing has priced itself out of all but a very small market. A two week pack trip for a family of four now costs a minimum of $1,000. Meanwhile some of the finest meadows in the Sierra were turned to deserts of sand, rocks and weeds, and campsites of spectacular beauty into dumps.

I would like to see the extension of the fixed camp with all accommodations, of the type now operated in Yosemite, to all the Sierra. It would be wonderful if all down the crest of the range, from Tuolumne Meadows to Mt. Whitney, and on in to Giant Forest, there were such camps, spaced an easy day's walk apart—say every nine miles.

There is plenty of room. They wouldn't have to be planted smack in the midst of the famous beauty spots, but as they are in Yosemite, just a little out of the way, beside the trail.

Such a program would make trips possible for thousands of people who now find it too difficult or too expensive to enjoy the exhilarating and healing beauty of the high country, and it would put a stop to uncontrolled destructive grazing.

Of course, those who wanted to could still ride or knapsack or go with donkeys—but how many of California's present inhabitants know which end of a horse animal is the steering gear? How many can carry a 60 pound pack over mountain trails?

Trouble is, even now, heavily used, established for many years, the Curry Company's camps don't make money—and the capital

outlay for new ones has become fantastic. The Rockefellers and
Fords are always fretting about conservation—here's a chance to
achieve some big results with, in their terms, a minuscule outlay
of money.

JULY 8, 1962

Back up in the mountains on a pack trip with my two daughters, I
find myself thinking of the difficulties in the way of getting proper
recreational use of the Sierra Nevada wilderness areas.

The season is too short and the capital outlay too great for
pack outfits to make substantial profits. In addition, the overhead
is tremendous.

The days are gone when the cowboy used to say, "I'll work
fourteen hours a day, three hundred and sixty five days a year for a
dollar a day, but by gum, the rest of the time's my own." Nowadays
they get high wages. All the horses must carry heavy insurance,
whether they are working or not, camp cooks are almost unobtain-
able, and it's a long time since the Forest or Park Services have been
giving away the country for free.

Although prices are many times what they were when, as a
boy, I worked as a packer, the demand is still there. But the work
and the return are so unsatisfactory that it's a declining business.

It's too bad, because this is all the taste of the Old West any-
body but a few cowboys in Wyoming and Montana is ever likely to
get nowadays. I have gone in the mountains every summer since I
first came west 37 years ago. My daughters have had their birthdays
on pack trips except when we were in Europe. I guess it will last
my time, but it is a dying sport.

What will take its place? At present there are hundreds of sec-
tions in Sequoia-Kings River National Park which are never visited

over periods of 10 years. Traffic is too heavy along the main trails;
other areas, equally beautiful, have been visited only by the original
surveyors.

Suppose this is all opened up to helicopter? The Sonora Pass
region is the finest high mountain country immediately accessible
to San Francisco. What will happen if it is possible to leave the city
and be established in a camp at a lake in Emigrant Basin in a matter
of minutes?

Still in America we have wildernesses larger than many Euro-
pean countries. Here our civilization which is getting further and
further from its roots in nature can literally re-create itself, on skis in
winter, with a trout rod in summer, with a rifle in autumn. There's
only one trouble. More and more people need recreating. Not only
that, but they demand it and can afford it.

As it is now, what the head shrinkers call their case load is more
than the State and National Park and the National Forest Services
can handle. It is a case load too, and they are engaged in an essential
activity of public health. Yet many wilderness regions of the United
State get less money from the public purse now than they did 40
years ago. I know dozens of important trails in the mountains that
have not been repaired since the Three C boys went through in
the '30s.

What will happen when we stop making bombs and devote
the money to life enhancement instead of destruction? Unless we
are very careful, we'll just transport our problems from the Western
Addition to the shores of Lake Tahoe.

Another thing that has occurred to me on this trip is the
changing pattern of vacations themselves. They too are yielding to
group dynamics. Friends of mine have taken over the old Straw-
berry Hotel in the Sonora Pass country. They plan to run it as a
hostel for group conferences, seminars, even possibly musical and
art gatherings. What this is planned to be is a kind of poor man's

Aspen. Funding Aspen cost Walter Paepcke a vast pot of money. Now the idea is catching on as a feasible commercial proposition.

Nobody will ever make a fortune at it, but it's fun to run, and, as the fellow said, you meet such a nice class of people.

This is the same scheme as Mike Murphy has at Big Sur Hot Springs, where I was before Easter. I know, cynics say, "What are people going to do with all this leisure? Mot of them will just get drunk or watch television or both."

As a matter of fact, some of them are apparently going to start acting like Socrates and his friends, and others are going to make a modest competence taking care of them while they do. Some of the human race behave quite nicely if given a chance.

JULY II, 1962

We had a fine time in the mountains. At first we were going to pack out, but the boss packer where we stopped was, as they say, a doubtful quantity at best, so we went over to Tuolomne Meadows and stayed in the auto camp and hiked all over the Sierra uplands.

The peaks were still under snow, and the meadows were in the first flower of spring. This means of course that they were also full of mosquitoes, but then Sierra mosquitoes don't really know how to bite for keeps. The water was too high and there was too much feed (the mosquitoes) to fish. Nonetheless, we had one of the best times ever.

I know of few more beautiful mountain trips by car than the circuit, Sonora Pass, Bridgeport, Mono Lake, Lee Vining, Tioga Pass, Tuolomne Meadows. I once had an opportunity to settle in Bridgeport and I've always rather regretted that I didn't take it up. I wonder what kind of person I would have become?

It's one of the earth's more noble landscapes, the dark sedge meadows, and pale olive sagebrush plains and bare peaks of the intermountain country.

It always thrills me, in the spring of the year, to cross the Sierra and drop down through the perfumed air, picking up, one by one, the characteristic flowers of a biological province that stretches with little variation from Canada deep into Mexico. Prickly white poppies, large pale blue penstemon, blazing star, and pale blue Nevada iris in all the meadows, with the yellow headed blackbirds singing over them, and at night, the sky full of bull-bats, Texas nighthawks with their lonely piercing cry and the startling zoom of the wings as they dive and recover in their dance in the evening air.

Yes, maybe I should have stayed in Bridgeport. I might have become a character in an Ernest Haycock novel. There are worse fates. Probably though, I would have left and returned to San Francisco and in July 1962 would be writing a column about the beauties of the intermountain country. You can't fight City Hall.

AUGUST 26, 1962

SEQUOIA NATIONAL PARK—That could be the dateline on half my books. Those that weren't written here were mostly written in a cabin in Devil's Gulch in Marin County, now an abandoned ruin in Samuel Taylor State Park. That was a lovely place, built above two waterfalls, like Frank Lloyd Wright's Falling Waters, a 10 foot square hut buried in a canyon in the middle of three abandoned ranches. Progress caught up with me and the greater good of the greater number evicted me. Now I'm middle aged and write in civilized surroundings.

It's 35 years since I first saw the Kings River Canyon and the headwaters of Kern River and caught my first Golden Trout. Progress has caught up with me here too, but not to the same degree. I went in over the same trails, serviced by the same pack outfits, as

Jack London and George Sterling and Jimmie Hopper and Stewart
Edward White. Clarence King came this way, and John Muir, Wil-
liam Randolph Hearst Sr., too. This is the classic High Sierra of
California tradition.

In those days there was no road into the Kings Canyon and only
a steep, hot, gravel road straight up into Giant Forest. There was
no High Sierra Trail and the John Muir Trail was still full of gaps.
The way into the country was either through Hume Lake, then a
shambles of a deserted logging village, or Mineral King, a mining
camp which was turning into a summer resort. The country was
more or less run by a small collection of outrageous characters, Cali-
fornia mountain men the like of which there will never be again.

There was the packer who controlled the Kings Canyon traffic,
Poly (for Napoleon) Kanawyer, a little wild man who rode like the
Tatar invasion, drank like Jonah's whale and hunted like Nimrod
himself.

His father had preceded him, and developed the first resort in
the Canyon, the site of which still bears his name. Past 80, Poly's
mother was washed away fording Kings River, got to her horse's
head, swam him out and showed up in camp a little late, apologetic
for the delay—"I got a little wet crossing the river." All the Val-
ley papers came out with editorials bemoaning the passing of the
virtues of the pioneer woman. And they were so right.

There was Shorty Lovelace, an even smaller, even wilder man,
who trapped along the border of the park, the watershed of the
Kings and Kaweah Rivers, in the winter, and guided hunters and
fishermen in the summer. I first came on him in Big Arroyo, on
horseback, a fly rod in either hand, drunker than a peach orchard
boar, hooting and hollering, and flipping fish out on the bank for
the dudes, as fast as he could flip.

One spring he showed up in civilization with a bad limp.
"Broke the ball and socket out of my hip." "What did you do?"

"Crawled with the snowshoes to the cabin, set it and laid out till it got well." I think they sent him up for poaching in his extreme old age. Now his base cabins on Sugarloaf Creek are tumbled ruins, lonelier than Karnak or Baalbek.

Over in the Kern the men were even harder, but quieter, steely eyed Nevada desert types with spotted calf hides covering their pack boxes, pinto horse-hide chaps and stock that would jump three feet in the air every time you coughed. All along the Kings upland were summer camps of cattle outfits. I knew them all—Cutlers, Bartons, Crabtrees, Goyens. They are all gone now and the Park has closed out their claims.

Only an old lady lingers on. Every summer she still comes up to Horse Corral Meadow. There's a roadhead there now, at least an appallingly bad road gives up at that point, and all sorts of comings and goings. The barbecues when everybody got together at fall gathering are long gone, and Old Ike, with his drooping moustaches and his little fox terrier riding across his saddle, is only a ghost on the trail now.

The High Sierra are getting civilized—or at least Los Angelized. Here and there the old-timers linger on and in fact are breeding new timers like themselves. I don't know of any such in California, but the other day I was up in Oregon, visiting a big ranch that raises rodeo stock for most of the shows in the West.

The daughter said, "I'm not much of a rider. The other day I got over in a Cossack drag and the horse started to gallop too fast and I couldn't get back up. Gee, I sure got cussed out. I guess I'll never learn to ride." Hmmm. In my most reckless salad days you couldn't have got me to even try to learn a Cossack drag, not for all the rice in China. Try it some time, just for size.

JUNE 30, 1963

Thirty-five years ago or so I first started hiking around the long
high ridges and deep wooded valleys of northwestern Marin
County. Less than an hour's drive from the city, it is to this day
remarkably sparsely populated, a land of a few vast dairy farms, still
little changed by man. Several of my books were written in a cabin
in Devil's Gulch, buried in the dense woods on the west side of Mt.
Barnabe, beside a narrow waterfall.

Last week I stopped at the headquarters of Samuel Taylor State
Park to get permission to use the hikers' and riders' camp in Devil's
Gulch, which is not part of the park, and was amazed to see on a
large map—"Staircase Falls," "Rexroth Cabin." Well, well. Me and
John Muir. Not only that, but the Sierra Club had marked with
removable yellow plastic ribbons a hike to that very spot for the
coming weekend.

I walked to the waterfall while my little girls were fixing up
around the camp. The cabin had long since crumbled into ruins,
but nothing else was changed. All was just as it was the rainy au-
tumn evening in 1928 I first stumbled on this hidden cul de sac in
the steep forest. The little cabin was less than 10 feet square, hardly
bigger than its piled rock fireplace. The door was open, there were
pots and pans, an oil lamp, some old quilts hung up out of the way
of mice and wood rats, and a primitive shower bath built over the
stream. In the still autumn twilight, with the yellow maple leaves
falling over it, cabin, clearing and waterfall looked just slightly omi-
nous, like something in a fairy story.

I stayed the night, back then in 1928, and in the next few
months met most of the people who used the place. Nobody knew
who had built it.

Later in the next gully a somewhat more substantial cabin was
built by one of the groups that used the first place. It was consider-

ably larger and stood directly over the confluence of two cascades, like the retreat of some Japanese Buddhist saint. It still survives as a tumbled ruin.

In the course of time all the people who used either cabin drifted away or outgrew such activities, and I was left in sole possession. Twice during the war, when it was impossible to get to the Sierra, I spent the entire summer in the larger cabin. Whenever I had some thorny literary job to do, I would go over and work in solitude until it was done. Then the property became a State park and I was evicted.

Last week, sitting in a little patch of sunlight at the foot of the waterfall, I felt as though I might just have found the place a few minutes before. There was no mirror to show me my changed face or my gray hair. If I looked down at my body—it was dressed in just the same clothes—jeans, red shirt, ankle length boots. I thought over the long intervening years, that now seemed to have slipped by imperceptibly. Deaths and marriages, two children, 15 books, travel about the world—had the maple and Douglas fir beside the waterfall grown or decayed? Had the number of ferns increased?

Down below, along the main stream, things had changed. During the war the range was badly overgrazed and in a couple of years the water tore loose great trees along the banks, the meadow shores were changed to cobbles; thistles and poison hemlock grew everywhere. The damage of overgrazing is sudden and dramatic, the healing processes are slow indeed. However good care the park authorities take of the Devil's Gulch, I will never live to see it as once it was.

I sat by the waterfall and watched the golden laurel leaves spin down into the pool. A mourning dove moaned softly off in the woods, red tailed hawks screamed, playing together in the sky, a doe and two fawns crossed the clearing, unaware of my presence.

Had all those years really been? Maybe I had drowsed away in the warm sunlight and the sound of falling water and dreamed it all—the Depression, the War, books, paintings, girls, the achievements and troubles of a life. I looked behind me, the cabin certainly was gone; but when I looked at the wet greenish black cliff and twisting water I sank into their own timelessness.

At last the sunlight went away and it grew chilly. I got up and went down the steep trail, and back down the valley to the campground and my busy daughters. I was a little stiff—I must have sat too long by the waterfall.

AUGUST 18, 1963

Thirty-six years ago, one warm September day in the onset of autumn in the High Sierra, Andrée Rexroth and I first climbed up Bloody Canyon and over Mono Pass and saw stretched before us the vast meadow lands at the headwaters of the Tuolumne River. It is 26 years since she has been gone from the mountains we both loved so much, but I still go back to the same places—the Whitney Plateau, Tuolumne Meadows, Humphrey Basin, the Chagoopa Plateau, Lake Italy, Palisade Basin.

There are other spots almost as beautiful in the Sierra and I have seen all of them, but as time goes on the choice narrows, certain campsites have become a second home and I would feel lost if I was away from them for too long.

Some are hard to get to, too rough for horses or mules, and can be reached only with donkeys or on foot. In such places it is easy, not just to recapture the freshness of life of primitive man, but to fancy that you are a visitor from another planet in the days before mankind appeared on earth. Tuolumne Meadows is not at all remote, on the contrary, a high-gear, well-paved road runs straight across it. There is a store, a coffee shop, a tourist camp, a Curry

Company Lodge and a Sierra club camp and lodge.

Time was when all these people running about would have given me fits. I used to feel they were desecrating the pristine wilderness which would be saved entire for knapsackers like myself and my friends. This is still the attitude of many people who fancy themselves conservationists. I guess I am turning mellow, because I positively enjoy seeing crowds from the prairies of the Middle West and the streets of New York loose in the wilderness for the first time in their lives.

We just came back from an idle trip. We had no objectives, no campsites to reach by a certain hour, nothing to climb. We wandered around the miles and miles of meadow land with a couple of pet donkeys to carry our stuff. Some days we traveled only four miles, other days we didn't travel at all. We fished, swam in the icy water, or did nothing at all.

This isn't, as you might think, mellowing with age. I have climbed all sorts of things by all sorts of routes and scrambled over miles of rock with a rucksack on my back to reach some out of the way lake, and in other mountains chopped steps in glaciers for hours. But I am also a strong advocate of do nothing and always have been.

Years ago, before ever the road went into Kings River Canyon, Andrée and I learned from the convict camp of a trail unknown to packers and guides, much less to any dudes. We used to hike in to old "Put" Boyden's cabin and the cave that now bears his name, usually late in October, and drowse away the warm golden days alongside pools full of two foot trout as drowsy as we were.

"You who were a girl of silk and gauze are now my mountain and waterfall companion" said the poet Po Chu I in his old age. I translated the poem in my young days and was deeply moved, but I never thought that in my own middle age I too would have a young dancer to wander with me by the falling crystal waters and amongst the peaks of snow and granite, least of all that, unlike Po's girl, she should be my very daughter.

"Wild cyclamen blooms in the meadow. Trout veer in the transparent current. At night golden Scorpio curls above the glimmering ice field. The snow of a thousand winters melts in the sun of a summer day. A thousand birds sing in the sunrise. After twilight our campfire is a single light amongst the lonely mountains. The manifold voices of the cascade talk all night. Wrapped in their down bags the girls sleep in the starlight. Their breaths come and go in tiny pulsing clouds in the frosty night."

That's the way Po Chu I would have described it, and that is the way it was. It is not everybody whose life can sometimes match the most perfect expressions of art.

AUGUST 21, 1963

There came in the mail a folder from Trustees for Conservation, whose address is 251 Kearny St., in case you want to receive conservation material from them. They urge me to do something to help get the Wilderness Bill out of committee and onto the floor of the House. I am all for it. It's hard to see how anyone could be against it.

It would not close down any mine, stop any logging operation, cancel any grazing permit, or abrogate any valid mining claim. What it would do would be to coordinate the administration of the wilderness areas now divided between the Department of Agriculture and Interior, and draw guide lines for policy in the field of public interest where policy is not truly well defined and so is at the mercy of pressure, ignorance or minority interest.

I consider myself a strong conservationist yet I have been interested for years in extending the series of High Sierra camps of the type operated by the Curry Company in Yosemite. I'd like to see the number in that park doubled, and 10 new ones in Sequoia-Kings Canyon Park. This gives the strict interpretationers of the Sierra Club fits.

On the other hand, I'd like to forbid the grazing of pack stock in the national parks altogether—and begin with the Sierra Club High Trips. Instead, I think all freight transport for campers should be by air drop. This suggestion is met with profound silence from defenders of the wilderness who think that a five-minute flight by an airplane is a violation of nature, but 200 horses and mules for one outfit are not.

So you see, it's not just the old struggle between the sheep-herders and Gifford Pinchot. We need to clarify policy amongst ourselves—us conservationists.

Another proposal of Trustees for Conservation is a system of national recreation areas near to population centers. San Francisco has the Marin Water District, the Regional Parks, a number of State Parks and its own Crystal Springs Water District.

Many far larger cities than San Francisco have nothing at all. But the plank in the Ts for C program I'm most for is a revival of the CCC, a Young Conservation Corps to provide work in national parks, national forests and other wilderness and recreation areas. The comparison of world wide statistics shows conclusively that adolescent delinquency increases in direct proportion to lack of opportunity to do something useful. Let's hope it is bigger, better and more business-like than Roosevelt's venture. We certainly need it.

People are becoming redundant. There are no jobs for the minorities demanding job equality. The population of a whole state—West Virginia—is in danger of being swept under the rug as obsolete. The demands of the automobile take precedence over the amenities of human life in the planning of our cities. The aged are housed like criminals. A Youth Conservation Corps would conserve youth as well as nature, and youth, like old age, stoop labor and locomotive firemen, is in great danger of becoming redundant—and that before it ever gets started.

AUGUST 23, 1964

When you read this I will be far away in a tent in the High Sierras with my daughters, Mary and Katharine.

... People often speak of going into the wilderness to get away from it all. Maybe that is what I did when I was young, because I remember months together spent alone or with my first wife, Andrée, living out of a rucksack and seldom seeing anybody. The Sierras were less used then and it was easier to do.

We spent our time in meditation and wonder—climbing is an exercise of wonder and fishing is an exercise of meditation—gathering our strength from within ourselves. When we would see people in the distance, we would avoid them, and we were always irritable when we had to come down for supplies and mix briefly with other humans.

I guess that is what age does, what they call maturing, because now my motives seem to me quite the opposite. I go to the mountains not to get away from it, but to get with it. As 11 months roll by I feel myself getting more and more mechanical in my attitude towards other men. Imperceptibly men take on the masks and costumes of causes and tendencies, and classes and forces and ideologies and all the false faces of generalization with which we classify human beings.

The most mortal of sins, said Immanuel Kant, is to consider another man as an instrument or a means and not as an end in himself. Yet our whole society strives, inhumanly and insensibly, to make instruments of us all, one to the other. We are all corrupted by a

world in which everything and everyone is a means to something
else. I resist it always, but it creeps over me like an infection, the virus
that turns each other man, himself an "I" like myself, into a thing in
my eyes—and so secretly turns me slowly to a thing likewise.

So if I go away for a little and associate with rocks and stars and
flowers and fish, the living perspective comes back. Alice over in
Africa, the President in the White House, the murderer on Death
Row, the Pope in the Vatican, the people that pass in the street—
they cease to represent anything but themselves—human like my-
self. They aren't Marxists or Catholics or Democrats or Americans
or Eskimos or Negroes. They're just like me. We're all here together
and we don't know what's going to happen next.

... It is August, and as I lie under the sky of late summer and
watch the Great Nebula of Andromeda swim past overhead—a
cloud of millions of stars all as big as our sun—I think of the world
down below the mountains. There are over 2 billion men out there.
Each one of them is an animal like me, naked under his clothes.
Under his skin his body is full of blood and bones and meat and
mysterious capsules and sponges which hold his life. Sometimes
these things hurt him and one day they stop working and he dies
and decays away. He doesn't represent anything except himself, a
self called Barry or Nikolai or Wang or Nkekerere. There will never
be another one like him. Each one of him swims by my imagination
like the Andromeda Nebula, a 2-billion-fold cloud, and each one
of him says to me the word that denies absolutely that he can ever
be a thing, the word I call myself—"I."

DECEMBER 2, 1964

We went up to Yosemite for the Thanksgiving weekend, as I have
been doing, unless I was in Europe, for time out of mind. We had

dinner with friends who are long time residents of Yosemite Val-
ley—French cuisine, candlelight and fine wine amongst the cliffs
and waterfalls. After dinner I read aloud a few of the many poems
I have written in the Sierra.

1927—thirty-seven years ago! Andrée Rexroth and I, new
come to California on our honeymoon, hitch-hiked up to Yo-
semite for Thanksgiving. We camped out against the sunny rocks
back of the Indian Village. Striped skunks and ringtailed cats came
and sat around our campfire. Gathering apples in the old orchard,
Andrée stepped on a drowsy bear. We roasted a chicken and baked
a cake in a reflector oven made of rocks. It was a fig cake. On the
way up we'd camped under a massive black fig tree, with the late
lingering fruit half dry on the branches and sweeter than sugar.

The same stars are still rising over the waterfalls, obedient to
the order of the year. I am grizzled and, as poets go, very success-
ful. My daughter and my secretary scramble up and watch the
water-rockets shoot down from Nevada Falls. Mary chatters about
her ballet and I think anew of Po Chu I's poem, "You who were
recently a creature of silks, gauze and satin have now become my
mountain and waterfall companion."

We didn't sleep out in a warm cove of the cliffs. On the con-
trary, we stayed in the luxurious new motel buildings at Yosemite
Lodge and ate turkey and drank champagne in our suite with a view
of the falls, the dark pines, the golden oaks, with the new snow
stretching underneath and out over the meadows.

Late Thanksgiving night I walked out across the meadow and
down to the river. The snow sparkled and creaked underfoot and
the stars shone up from the surface of the sliding, hissing water.

The next day a young bear who didn't have sense enough to
hibernate came, flopping his feet like Charlie Chaplin, through the
snow to investigate Carol—to her great delight.

A few minutes later, here came a coyote, big as a small Alsatian, all decked out in his new thick blue-gray winter furs. All in all—the Valley was at its best and seemed to be trying hard to please us.

And—more than all in all—levels of my mind came awake that had grown lethargic amongst the distractions of the city. I translated twelve poems of Pierre Reverdy's from the French and wrote some notes for some of my own and did a lot of pondering, mulling over and meditating. And the girls had a good time, too.

SEPTEMBER 13, 1965

Last week I was away, in a cabin deep in the woods, recollecting myself. No papers. No radio. No phone number. I go away as often as I can, which is not very often. Sometimes I write. Mostly I don't even think. I just contemplate—the forest, the world beyond it, myself, or the object of contemplation that comes when the mind empties itself of itself. Sometimes all existence seems to slip into focus. All its violence and tragedy and disorder take on a form and meaning that the mind can grasp briefly. Then the turmoil of existence seems a matter of scarcely perceptible changes of phase, like an ever so slightly varying colored light shifting over an immense diamond.

... What holds a civilization together, and makes the difference between creative growth and decay? What is the foundation that underlies and sustains all the activities of a people and energizes and forms that special unity we call culture? Peace. The peace which comes from the habit of contemplation. It is not intellectual knowledge of the unity of human endeavor, nor a philosophical notion of the ultimate meaning of the universe. It is an inward sense and an abiding quality of life, a temper of the soul. It is not rare nor hard to find. It offers itself at moments to everyone, from early childhood on, although less and less often if it is not welcomed. It can be seized and trained and cultivated until it becomes a constant habit in the background of daily life. Without it life is only turbulence, from which eventually meaning and even all intensity of feeling die out in tedium and disorder.

JANUARY 24, 1966

... With ever-increasing frequency, for the past few years, in San Francisco, in the Bay Area, in California, and all over the country, the small and embattled forces trying to stave off the destruction of a decently habitable environment have been faced with the technique of the massive, irreversible accomplished fact, with blitzkrieg, schrecklichkeit and efficient and plausible third column takeover.

Ecology, the relations of living species to one another and their environment, is precisely the field that lends itself best to irreversible processes—except maybe chemistry. The redwood forests of coast and sierra can no more be restored, for instance, than can the firecrackers of Chinatown's New Year celebration be uncracked.

The rapidity with which we are creating an environment in which the human species as we know it can no longer thrive is astonishing. We have passed, in California, a critical point. The resilience of the environment is exhausted, it can no longer recuperate from large-scale destruction in less than many centuries.

The forces that stand to profit from destruction now know this and they have learned to move quickly, on the largest possible scale, and if it can be managed, with an elaborate public relations camouflage which disguises them as "conservationists."

Once the forest cover of the Northern California streams is destroyed, flood, fire and erosion quickly create an irreversible situation. The topsoil is out in the Pacific Ocean or clogging the larger streams and we are not all that technologically advanced that we can put it back.

The Walt Disney development of Mineral King—far in excess of the Forest Service specifications—will be like a nuclear explosion in the heart of the finest mountain wilderness in California. Disney anticipates two and a half million visitors by 1976.

It was possible to put Nagasaki and Hiroshima back together again—give or take a few dead humans. Once gone, the wilderness is gone forever.

SEPTEMBER 11, 1966

.... We have reached the tipover point. The man-made environment is so vast that nature survives only in small islands, threatened constantly by biological changes from outside even under ideal conditions of protection.

We hold this land in trust for the 350,000 generations still, D.V., to come, barring our own passion for self-destruction.

Contact with the environment from which he came is strong medicine for the preservation of the species of man, it recreates him in the true sense, and it may well be essential for his survival.

We may discover that once we are all living in Megalopolis under a Dymaxion roof, we simply will start to die off.

Certainly the urban centers of the past, far less artificial, have never replenished themselves except by immigration from the countryside.

A virgin redwood forest, an unpolluted Lake Baikal, may be like hormones, tiny particles of the face of the globe, without which we cannot go on living.

From Rexroth's newspaper columns in the *San Francisco Bay Guardian*

DECEMBER 1969

The sudden tremendous interest in ecology among students, and in Berkeley and San Francisco amongst older people, and spreading across the country like wildfire, is not a fad, and it is not unheralded. For years, KPFA and the other Pacifica stations and their associates have hammered on the subject. On my own book review program, the oldest thing on the station, I have talked about it at every opportunity. Twenty-five years ago a group of us were conducting lectures and seminars at the Workman's Circle, whose whole emphasis was on ecology as a scientific foundation for a philosophy of social reorganization. The period of David Brower's leadership of the Sierra Club witnessed an attempt to turn that organization of Sunday hikers and summer trippers into the leading cadre of an ecological revolution—which is why he was ganged up on by corporation lawyers, power company executives, and Native Sons and Daughters of the Berkeley Hills.

The reason for the sudden explosion of the ecological revolution in the Bay Area is simple. It was prepared by many years of work, and it is occurring at the critical point when the ecology of California has become intolerable. Water turns into steam very suddenly; just as suddenly we have been brought face to face with the question, in the words of Lawrence Halprin, "Is man merely a dominant species in a transitional life association or is he the characteristic member of a climax of living things that will endure for a geological epoch or more?" The cockroaches and the octopuses are waiting. Perhaps we cannot turn the steam back into water. Perhaps the critical point is gone.

... The sudden popularity of ecology is not a craze. It is the response to the deadly crisis caused by a craze called the profit system. Man's end is in sight. One thing ecology has always taught is that the relationships of living things to each other and their environment are governed by critical points, where catastrophe occurs with great suddenness.

MAY 1969

In the past, men have planned utopias where life would be better, and they have advocated revolution to get rid of the predators of society and bring about a world where man was no longer wolf to man. Meanwhile, the human race struggled on, crippled and thwarted by exploitation and its side effects, from alcoholism to silicosis, but it survived.

For the last 200 years we have seen the growth of an economic and social system based fundamentally on the extractive industries and with a built-in dynamism that forces it into ever-increasing production at all costs. This competitive system has universalized a morality based on covetousness. For the last 50 years, the benefits, such as they are, of this system have been extended to most of the productive workers of the major industrial countries, the "metropoles." This is least true of the United States where about a tenth of the population is redundant—youth, the aged, Negroes, Southern poor whites and others. This is not due to the backwardness of the American economy; quite the contrary.

We have just gone through a long boom period with ever-accumulating surpluses; yet the overall production has never passed 80 percent of capacity. The source of profit is no longer, as it was in Marx's day, labor power. Every year we need fewer people to produce more. The surplus we lock up in subsidized housing projects, in Aid to Dependent Children or in Garrison State College or toss in the Disposall of Vietnam. Our social-economic structure is itself in a state of civil war. The old extractive, industrial, financial structure based ultimately on the exploitation of labor power applied directly to primary raw materials is at war with the new technological society of computers and transistors and the Keynesian morality of Hugh Hefner's *la vie luxueuse.* Meanwhile, outside the metropoles, starvation, disorder, breakdown sweep over the southern three-quarters of the globe.

Twenty-five years ago all the contradictions and conflicts of the present had already come into existence, but they only threatened individual men with war, hunger, and crippled lives. Today, an extractive, accumulative society more than just threatens—makes certain—the extinction of the human species within a comparatively short time.

The carbon dioxide content of the atmosphere can no longer be kept in balance even over the equatorial regions. A dense fog of carcinogens blankets whole areas.... The things we are doing to our environment are changing it far more drastically than the changes necessary to account for the extinction of the great reptiles at the end of the Jurassic Age and incomparably more quickly.

I have quoted before the old, now-abandoned slogan of the U. S. Forest Service: "The forest is a crop, not a mine." Unless we can stop treating the planet as a mine and start treating it as a crop, people now living will see the beginning of the end of the human species.

What can we do about it? Probably very little, because the old order is shutting down with a police state. In the Thirties the Marxists call Fascism and Nazism "forced rationalization" of the German and Italian economies. (Lenin admitted that Bolshevism was precisely forced rationalization.) Today, the state, but most especially the American state, is dedicated to forced irrationalization. Unless this can be halted, there is no hope for the human race. But what does this mean? It means de-mounting the whole structure, rebuilding it and starting in the opposite direction. Growth rates and GNPs and capital expansion have got to be replaced by changing the standard-of-living value system so that the possession of large numbers of commodities becomes a vice, not a virtue.

The extractive industries must be reduced to a minimum. The use of fossil fuels must be brought to a complete stop; coal, oil and gas should be consumed totally with nothing but completely inert residues at the sites and sent out over wires. Atomic plants should be stopped until it can be determined how to destroy the wastes. More and more articles should be made of organic plastics. Chemical fertilizers and insecticides must be replaced by organic manures, which now pollute all our bodies of water instead of being pumped into the fields, and by the ecological management of the health of agricultural crops; for instance, replacing poison sprays with ladybird beetles. There are innumerable ecological maneuvers of this kind now known. Along with this would have to go a complete moral conversion from the acquisitive, competitive, covetous "virtues" of present society to a whole new scale of cooperative mutual aid simplicity value system not unlike the South Sea Islanders of romance. The population growth must not just be stopped, but reversed. The optimum is probably about one billion people to the planet.

You say this sounds like turning the whole world into a national park? Precisely. We must save ourselves as we are trying to save the sandhill crane. All power to David Brower!

CORRESPONDENCE
& COMMENTARY

From Kenneth Rexroth and James Laughlin: Selected Letters (1939–1981)

LAUGHLIN TO REXROTH, JUNE 15, 1937

Dear Rexroth,

In spite of your last letter saying that you are going up into the Sierras before my arrival I still hope that you will break a toenail or something and will be still in San Francisco when I get there....

REXROTH TO LAUGHLIN, OCTOBER 21, 1939

.... How far away the mountains seem. Even more so when one is in them these days. I have been doing a lot of climbing this fall—every piton I drive in is like a fond kiss at the station as the troop train pulls out. Still, good climbing technique should be handy in and around Leavenworth. Unfortunately, I am not good enough with my flutterkick to ever get away from Alcatraz. Marie and I have talked seriously of going to Bolivia, where we want to go anyway—but I am afraid I am too deep in this thing to take a powder. I would let down too many people....

REXROTH TO LAUGHLIN, MAY 3, 1941

... Skiing? We took a long trip late last year, camped on the snow for 14 days the first hitch, 10 the second. Made several nice climbs and gave the iceaxe some work for a change. (The Sierras are mostly rockclimbs in the summer.) Terribly poor this year but I hope to make a trip along the Sierra summit from Carson Pass to Senora [*sic*] or Tioga Pass sometime this month.

LAUGHLIN TO REXROTH, MAY 16, 1945

Dear Kenneth,

I too am sad to miss the Sierra trip, but life seems to hem in more and more. I don't think we'll even get close to Jackson as the children are always sick or the nurse is sick or there is some reason to stay home and fuss.

But don't be downhearted, there will be better times later on.

REXROTH TO LAUGHLIN, APRIL 13, 1948

Dear Jim,

GOT GUG. Thank you for the good word. Now maybe I can afford a trip East this Fall. I think I will use it to live in the mountains for two years. I have it all planned. Altho I just planned it—I never expected to get a Guggenheim. It is good it came—because I need money so badly—now I can get necessary dental and medical work done too. . . .

REXROTH TO LAUGHLIN, JUNE 25, 1948

. . . . When, if ever, are you coming to the mountains (with) me?

    c̄ love KENNETH

LAUGHLIN TO REXROTH, DECEMBER 17, 1981
(last letter of the exchange):

Dear Kenneth—
I'm glad that we came by to see you, even though it was sad to see
you so reduced. I remembered our trips in the Sierras and our rock
climbing when you were in prime form. But I remembered what
you told me when Aunt Leila was ill, that I didn't understand the
will to live, and I think you have got that, and you will make it back
to health. You've just got to want to, and all of us are wishing for
you to do that. So keep working at it and get back to the speech
therapy when you can. You aren't any worse off than Bill Williams
was and he made it back.

From The Way It Wasn't, by James Laughlin (2006)

Kenneth Rexroth knew everything and would tell you about it. He had a photographic memory. After lunch he would lie in his bathtub for two hours, doing some light reading like the history of Chinese science.

■

The clarity of the stars seen through tent flaps. Rexroth and I often went camping in the Sierras. As we walked along he would explain all the flora and the geology. He was the best camp cook I ever knew; he could make delicious meals out of things that were light to pack. The master of tomato paste. He always took short pack rods. He could see a trout under the water thirty feet away. He knew the names of all the stars and the myths that went with them. One of our best trips was in late spring but there was still plenty of snow. We climbed in on skis from Bishop on the eastern slope. We camped near a frozen lake. He dug a berth in a snowbank with a ski end and bedded it with fir boughs. He really didn't care much about skiing. He just liked to be in the mountains. Next day I climbed up a big ridge, but he sat all day on a stump—it was sunny—meditating. I looked back down on him every now and then and he never changed his position for three hours.

One year we made the mistake of taking girls along, up King's River Canyon [*sic*]. He brought a poesy-loving coed from San Francisco State and I brought Henry Miller's crazy friend Elena ... taking the girls was an error. We took a burro that trip to pack the grub and tents and sleeping bags, but the city girls got sore feet and were miserable. Also they didn't like each other. By the time we came down nobody was speaking.

■

Kenneth sure had a messed up life. A wonder he accomplished as much as he did.

Dear Delmore,

I really think Rexroth is one of the most superior humans alive. He reminds me extensively of Wheelwright—a Wheelwright without psychic kinks. R. seems to enjoy life. A vast store of anecdotes delivered in an intermountain drawl. We spent Easter rock climbing down in the mountains and you have no idea how near you were to coming into your small fortune. We did a small, very vertical chimney and on the way down my extremities became completely dissociated from the petrous substance. Fortunately the sovietic bard was belaying me with his rope from above and by intellectual ruggedness maintained me in the air, for all the world as Virgil, to whom my poetry has so often been compared, would say, like the wily spider dangling from his self-begotten silky cord, until I retrenched myself in the rock.

From Byways, by James Laughlin (2005)

From PROLOGUE—THE NORFOLK SANTA—DAWN

Often now as an old man
Who sleeps only four hours a night,
I wake before dawn, dress and go down
To my study to start typing:
Poems, letters, more pages
In the book of recollections.

. . .

What is this line I'm writing?
I never could scan in school.
It's certainly not an Alcaic.
Nor a Sapphic. Perhaps it's
The short line Rexroth used
In *The Dragon and the Unicorn*,
Tossed to me from wherever
He is by the Cranky Old Bear
(but I love him).

THE OLD BEAR: KENNETH REXROTH

Sometimes he could be sweet as
Honey, but other times he was
Unbearably cranky; you couldn't
Get near him or he'd growl or
Even bite. People either loved
Him or thought he was bad news
And to be avoided at all costs.

That summer when I drove down
From Alta to visit him in San
Francisco he was on a roll of
Good humor and I found him
Quite irresistible. Many of
His stories were made up,
Obvious fictions of a wild
Imagination, but so funny
One wanted to believe them.
When it was time for New
Directions to publish his
Autobiography the lawyer for
The libel-insurance company
Read the script and was
Horrified. "You and this man
Will spend the rest of your
Lives in court." We solved
That problem by changing
Names of the characters who
Would be easy to identify
And making the title *An
Autobiographical Novel.*

. . .

Was another inspiration. They
Were deep in modernism. In 1935
The New Deal's WPA programs for
Artists and writers appealed to
Them as relief for the jobless
But even more politically. They
Were radicals: not communists
But anarchists. Kenneth's
Grandfather had been a friend

Of Eugene Debs, who went to
Jail for building up unions.
Kenneth had been raised on
Proudhon and Bakunin. Andrée
Was a feminist, one of her
Idols was Rosa Luxemburg, the
German revolutionary. Working
Together they did a 100-foot
Mural for a San Francisco
Health center, and Kenneth
Helped edit the California
Guidebook that the WPA
Sponsored. He was an ecologist
Ahead of his time.

Kenneth Rexroth, Observer, by Carter Scholz (2012)

As an amateur astronomer, I flinch when a poet looks up, or pretends to. Robert Frost, the ranking pretend astronomer among poets, observed, "Orion always comes up sideways / Throwing a leg up over our fence of mountains / And rising on his hands." And that is generally as good as it gets after dark with the poets. Very little is up to Robert Skelton's "Garland of Laurel."* More usually a planet, star, constellation, or the Moon is invoked as an ornament, sentiment, vague metaphor, or for the sonority of its name.

Kenneth Rexroth (1905–1982) is a strong exception. When he looks at the sky, he troubles to carefully observe what he's seeing, and to find the language to record it.

Rexroth's poems are often set in California's Sierra Nevada range, where I've backpacked for thirty years. I can say from my own experience that his descriptions are as solid as any I've read, including John Muir's. I was particularly struck when Kim Stanley Robinson sent me a photo he'd taken while backpacking near Deadman Pass. The day before, I'd happened to read "Toward an Organic Philosophy," in which Rexroth describes a red cliff:

---

* Skelton's poem begins,
>   Arectyng my syght towarde the zodyake,
>   The sygnes xii for to beholde a farre,
>   When Mars retrogradant reuersyd his bak,
>   Lord of the yere in his orbicular,
>   Put vp his sworde, for he cowde make no warre,
>   And whan Lucina plenarly did shyne,
>   Scorpione ascendynge degrees twyse nyne.

This conjunction of Mars retrograde and the Moon in the eighteenth degree of Scorpius has been dated to May 8, 1495. See Gingerich, O. & Melvin J. Tucker, "The Astronomical Dating of Skelton's *Garden of Laurel*," *Huntington Library Quarterly*, v.32, n.3, University of California Press, 1969.

I would be unsurprised to learn that Rexroth knew this poem.

The lowest meadow is a lake,
The next two are snowfields, the pass is covered with snow,
Only the steepest rocks are bare. Between the pass
And the last meadow the snowfield gapes for a hundred feet,
In a narrow blue chasm through which a waterfall drops,
Spangled with sunset at the top, black and muscular
Where it disappears again in the snow.
The world is filled with hidden running water
That pounds in the ears like ether;
The granite needles rise from the snow, pale as steel;
Above the copper mine the cliff is blood red,
The white snow breaks at the edge of it.

I stared at the photo for a few seconds and said, "That's the place."
And so it was.

Rexroth was an autodidact, and a public figure. As such,
he was perhaps especially careful about policing and proving the
boundaries of his knowledge. In astronomy he was conversant with
some star names, some constellation figures, eclipses, planetary
conjunctions, and some naked-eye deep space objects, including
the Messier objects M31, M13, M44 and M42 (the Andromeda
galaxy, the Great Globular Cluster in Hercules, the Beehive Open
Cluster in Cancer, and the Orion Nebula). They're described in
his sequence "The Lights in the Sky Are Stars" (titled after a line by
Archibald MacLeish). After reading these I believed his observations
of the night sky were as solid and recognizable as that red cliff.

Planetary motions are complex but regular. They make a reli-
able clock in the sky. Rexroth was so scrupulous an observer that
one can precisely date several poems containing astronomical ob-
servations, by using planetarium software. (I used Cartes du Ciel.)

I established a likely period of composition for each poem of
astronomical interest, based on publication dates. Rexroth was a
prolific writer throughout his life, and did not customarily revise

earlier work. I assumed that a poem in any particular book was written after the previous book was sent to press. Then I stepped the software through that period, looking for correspondences to his descriptions.

I found nine instances detailed enough to fix a date to them. A few were ambiguous, but those poems often contained other helpful chronology, such as the age of his daughter, or the season of the year. The source used for the texts and chronology was *The Complete Poems of Kenneth Rexroth* (Sam Hamill & Bradford Morrow, eds., Copper Canyon Press, 2003).

■

From "Toward an Organic Philosophy":

SPRING, COAST RANGE

> Scorpio rises late with Mars caught in his claw;
> The moon has come before them ...
> It is April ...
> Orion walks waist deep in the fog coming in from the ocean;
> Leo crouches under the zenith.

Mars is in Scorpius for some months every few years (Rexroth makes a common error in using the astrological name Scorpio), but the "claw" narrows it, and "April" confirms it. Since the moon comes "before" them, rather than nearer to Leo or Orion, the possible dates are limited to April 24 to 26, 1937. If Orion is setting into the ocean's fog, Mars has just risen, and the time is about 9:15 p.m. PST. Later in the same poem is this:

FALL, SIERRA NEVADA

> Ritter and Banner ...
> At sunset the half-moon rides on the bent back of the Scorpion,
> The Great Bear kneels on the mountain.
> Ten degrees below the moon
> Venus sets in the haze arising from the Great Valley.
> Jupiter, in opposition to the sun, rises in the alpenglow
> Between the burnt peaks.

Autumn oppositions of Jupiter—moments when the planet is exactly opposite the Sun in our sky—occurred in 1939 and 1940. Since this poem was published in 1940, that year is impossible, so the only possible autumn date is November 13, 1939, but it's most unlikely that Rexroth was in the High Sierra in mid-November. However, in 1938, Jupiter was in opposition on August 21. It's likely that Rexroth is using the term "opposition" loosely, and it's actually a month later, September 28, 1938. Everything else fits this date: the moon is 28% illuminated and close to the "back" of Scorpius, and Venus is fifteen degrees from the Moon. Sunset was about 5:40 p.m. PST. Alpenglow on the peaks would have continued another hour or more. At 7 p.m., Jupiter was at altitude 30 degrees, azimuth 144 degrees. If Ritter and Banner are the "burnt peaks" between which Jupiter rose, Rexroth's campsite that night was at Lake Catherine, from which the San Joaquin ("Great") Valley is also visible; from this vantage Ursa Major would have been "kneeling" above Mount Davis to the northwest.

From "Andrée Rexroth":

> The years have gone. It is spring
> Again. Mars and Saturn will
> Soon come on, low in the West,
> In the dusk.

In the spring of 1948, Mars and Saturn were in conjunction be-
tween Cancer and Leo. Their closest approach, to within about
three degrees of each other, was on March 30, 1948. However, they
would not be "low in the West / in the dusk" until late May or early
June, consistent with "... a long / Spring evening." (Another such
conjunction occurred in the spring of 1946, but Rexroth writes,
addressing his wife who died in 1940, "It is almost ten years since
... ") Later in the poem:

> The moon sinks through deep haze ...
> Saturn gleams through the thick light
> Like a gold, wet eye; nearby,
> Antares glows faintly,
> Without sparkle.

Rexroth mistakes Jupiter for Saturn. Saturn was not near Antares
any time between 1929 and 1956, but in the summer of 1948 Jupiter
was. For the Moon to be setting this early in the evening, it could
be July 9 to 11, 1948, or (given the High Sierra travel season) more
likely August 6 to 7, 1948. Jupiter through haze does in fact look
like a gold, wet eye.

From "Blood on a Dead World":

> A blowing night in late fall,
> The moon rises with a nick
> In it. All day Mary has
> been talking about the eclipse
> ... not
> That we expect a four
> Year old child to understand ...
> "The earth's shadow is like blood."

This lunar eclipse, on January 18, 1954, reached totality at 6:30 p.m. PST. The reddish shadow of Earth on the Moon occurs only at totality. Moonrise that day was 5:11 p.m., and the eclipse had already begun. Rexroth has misremembered the season, but the other details are correct. Mary is Rexroth's daughter, born in 1950.

■

From "Protoplasm of Light," in the longer sequence "The Lights in the Sky Are Stars":

> How long ago
> Frances and I took the subway
> To Van Cortlandt Park....

> Under
> The trees the sun made little
> Lunes of light through the bare branches
> On the snow....

> One by
> One the stars came out. At last
> The sun was only a thin
> Crescent in our glasses with the
> Bright planets nearby like watchers.

> Then the great cold amoeba
> Of crystal light sprang out
> On the sky. . . .

This passage describes a total eclipse of the Sun seen from the
Bronx, New York City, on January 24, 1925. The time of totality
was about 9:11 a.m. EST. The eclipse was total only in the north-
ernmost districts of the city. Rexroth has precisely described the
effect of the sun's shape; it is partially covered by the moon, and
diffracted by the trees upon the ground. There was indeed a striking
conjunction of three planets about twenty degrees west of the Sun:
Venus, Mercury, and Jupiter were all within three degrees of each
other. The "great cold amoeba" is the Sun's corona, visible only at
totality. Later in the same poem:

> Twilight comes and all of the
> Visible planets come out.
> Venus first, and then Jupiter,
> Mars and Saturn and finally
> Mercury once more. . . .

Rexroth describes another evening, one conjunction calling an-
other to mind. This part of the poem is addressed to his daughter
Mary, so it is unlikely to have been written before 1953, when she
was three. It was published in 1956. There is no year from 1953 to
1956 when all five "naked-eye" (Rexroth calls them "visible") plan-
ets were in the sunset sky, but there are two near-misses. Between
February 12 and March 12, 1953, all the planets but Saturn made a
striking cluster in the western sky, near the star Aldebaran, which
is approximately the brightness and color of Saturn. Rexroth might
have mistaken Aldebaran for Saturn. From February 14 to 26 the
Moon would have been prominent; its absence from the poem
argues against those dates. Also possible, though less likely, is May
16 to 31, 1954. The sticking point in this case is Mars, which rose

after Jupiter set. Rexroth might have mistaken Antares, rising in the east, for Mars, especially towards the end of this window of time, but this arrangement is not so striking.

■

From "Another Twilight":

> ... Venus and the transparent
> Crescent moon. Venus is caught
> In the Crab's claws, the moon creeps
> Between the Virgin's open thighs.

From July 25 to 27, 1952, Venus is in Cancer, and the Moon is in its crescent phase, moving into Virgo over these three nights. Another possible alignment of Venus in Cancer in this time period, June 14 to 28, 1954, is unlikely; it's too early in the season for a Sierra trip, and the Moon at that time is past crescent phase.

■

From "Yin and Yang":

> It is spring once more in the Coast Range
> Warm, perfumed, under the Easter moon.
> The flowers are back in their places....
> The Lion gives the moon to the Virgin.
> She stands at the crossroads of heaven,
> Holding the full moon in her right hand,
> A glittering wheat ear in her left.

This "Easter moon" (the full moon preceding Easter Sunday) was on March 27, 1964. But on that night Virgo no longer held the Moon in her "right hand," the arc between beta and gamma Virginis; by then it had moved to a position between her arms, near gamma. The "wheat ear" is often portrayed in antique illustrations of the constellation.

It's clear that Rexroth was an accurate observer and scrupulous re-
corder of the night sky. None of these excerpts failed to produce a
confirming date, even though in two of them there is an honest mis-
take. I find it almost a statement of poetic principle, the degree to
which Rexroth grounds these poems in observation and recording.
With this faith in reality is a faith in his readers. Probably not one in
a hundred readers would have known or cared if he'd been making
it up. He seems to have considered astronomy as a form of literacy,
which an educated person should know and honor. He would no
sooner slight its realities than he would misquote Shakespeare.

There's a species of modesty among amateur astronomers; in
deference to the professionals, they describe themselves as "observ-
ers." Kenneth Rexroth was just that, an observer.

NOTES

KENNETH REXROTH'S MOUNTAIN POETRY

CLIMBING MILESTONE MOUNTAIN, AUGUST 22, 1937
Milestone Mountain is a peak on Great Western Divide, a long
ridge that runs roughly parallel and to the west of the Sierra crest. A
prominent summit finger when seen from the east gives Milestone
Peak its name. Rexroth's climbing route was from the west, and is
now rated Class 3.

Ferdinando Nicola Sacco and Bartolomeo Vanzetti were an-
archists convicted of murder in a controversial trial. They were
executed in Boston on August 23, 1927. Twenty thousand gathered
on the Boston Commons to protest on the night of August 21.

The Marie here is Marie Kass, Rexroth's second wife. Their
first Sierra trip together took place in 1936.

NORTH PALISADE, THE END OF SEPTEMBER, 1939
North Palisade is the highest peak in the Palisades section of the
Sierra crest (14,242 feet). The easiest routes are Class 4, meaning
ropes are recommended for protection, but solo climbers usually
don't use them.

Rexroth references this trip in his letter of October 1939 to
James Laughlin (p. 177). The poem "Strength Through Joy" also
describes this trip.

HIKING ON THE COAST RANGE
Howard Sperry and Nick Bordoise were San Francisco workers
who joined the International Longshoremen's strike, which began
on May 9, 1934. They were killed on "Bloody Thursday," July 5,
1934, when police and others attacked the strikers. "Conderakis"
appears to be Rexroth's mistake. Rexroth was a member of the
National Maritime Union, which he had helped to organize. He
participated in demonstrations that were part of the maritime Gen-
eral Strike of July 16, 1934, called to protest police brutality.

ON WHAT PLANET
The Sierra Club's climbing classes in the late 1930s sometimes went
to Hunters Hill, near Vallejo and the intersection of Highways 80
and 37 just east of San Francisco Bay. This is one of the few Sierra
Club activities Rexroth admitted to joining.

TOWARD AN ORGANIC PHILOSOPHY
Spring, Coast Range
In 1928 Rexroth found and began to use an abandoned cabin in
Devil's Gulch on the north flank of Tamalpais in Marin Country,
as he describes in his *San Francisco Examiner* column of June 30,
1963 (p. 156).

Spring, Sierra Nevada
Deadman Canyon is a long glacial canyon running north to the
Kings River from the Kings-Kaweah Crest, which in Rexroth's
time was called the Silliman Crest (see map, pp. xvi–xvii). The pass
Rexroth refers to, now called Elizabeth Pass, is the subject of an early
Sierra book, *The Pass*, by Stewart Edward White, whom Rexroth
mentions in his *Examiner* column of August 26, 1962 (p. 156).

The copper mine was a brief venture in the 1880s of Judge
William Wallace of Fresno, working a tiny outcropping just under

Peak 12,345; Wallace later admitted it was mainly an excuse to spend his summers in the Sierra. The mine outcropping in sunset light is indeed "blood red."

Fall, Sierra Nevada
Banner and Ritter are twin peaks at the north end of the Minaret range, just southeast of Yosemite National Park. At 13,157 feet, Ritter is the tallest peak in the Yosemite region. Looking up the V between the two suggests Rexroth was camped at Lake Catherine.

The White Mountains are the range paralleling the Sierra Nevada to the east, on the other side of the Owens Valley (see map, pp. xx–xxi).

John Tyndall (1820–1893), a prominent Victorian scientist, did work in chemistry and geology, and was a noted mountaineer (he made the first ascent of the Weisshorn in the Swiss Alps). Of his seventeen books, the likeliest source for the sentences Rexroth quotes is *The Glaciers of the Alps*, 1860.

VALUE IN MOUNTAINS
This poem and the two that follow, "A Lesson in Geography" and "Ice Shall Cover Nineveh," are examples of what Rexroth called his "Cubist" poetry. In the 1930s Rexroth was powerfully impressed by the philosophy of Alfred North Whitehead and the art of Pablo Picasso and Gertrude Stein. He experimented for a while with a poetic form in which each line or phrase takes a different angle on the subject of the poem, creating a disjunctive succession of phrases and ideas, unlike his more usual conversational style. Rexroth's biographer Rachelle Lerner has written very helpfully about these Cubist poems.

A LESSON IN GEOGRAPHY
Sir John Mandeville is the supposed author of *The Travels of Sir John Mandeville*, published in Anglo-Norman around 1357.

The Wabash River is the largest river in Indiana, which was briefly Rexroth's childhood home.

Kōjō n'suki ("The Moon over the Ruined Castle") is a Japanese song of the Meiji Period, written by Rentaro Taki in 1901.

Cynoglossum is a forget-me-not with a particular shade of blue, and is also a name for the herb, hound's tongue.

ICE SHALL COVER NINEVEH
Section 3: The Tablelands is the name of a plateau at the western end of the Kings-Kaweah Divide (Silliman Crest), and everything in this section is congruent with the place in the 1930s, when sheep were still allowed to graze there.

From IN THE MEMORY OF ANDRÉE REXROTH
This is an excerpt from a longer poem, the first of five poems Rexroth wrote in memory of his wife Andrée Rexroth after her death in 1940. All of them are also mountain poems, although the least so is this first poem in the sequence; the mountain allusions are all confined to Part c, "a time," which is included here. Rexroth and Andrée met in 1926 when Rexroth was twenty-one and Andrée twenty-four. They married the next year, and soon after, settled in San Francisco and started making trips into the Sierra. They continued to go up there frequently until 1935, when Andrée's epileptic seizures and the pressures of their bohemian lifestyle caused them to separate.

NIGHT BELOW ZERO
From many points in the Sierra Nevada, even on the Sierra crest, one can see west all the way down to California's Great Central Valley, and on clear days across the valley to the coast range.

STRENGTH THROUGH JOY

This is another poem from the fall of 1939. The "col between Isosceles Peak and North Palisade" is now called Thunderbolt Pass, a Class 2 pass providing access between Dusy Basin and Palisades Basin (see map, pp. xx–xxi). From the pass, one can see down the length of the range to the southeast. The Whitney pluton is exceptionally white granite, and the Kaweahs are a ridge to the west of Whitney, made of a roof pendant of red metamorphic rock.

The German Paul Bauer led two expeditions to Kanchenjunga in 1929 and 1931. Bill Tilman and Eric Shipton were British climbers and explorers who made several reconnaissance expeditions in the Himalayas. Frank Smythe's vision occurred in 1924, during the last Mallory expedition to the north side of Everest; Smythe made a solo climb up the Northern Couloir and experienced a persistent sense that a second climber was following him. The incident became famous, and was referenced by T. S. Eliot in his poem "The Wasteland" ("who is the third who walks always beside you?").

The "mad children of the Eigerwand" refers to the many attempts during the 1930s to climb the north wall of the Eiger in the Swiss Alps; several of these resulted in fatal accidents. Toni Kurz froze at the end of his rope in 1936, the last of his team of four to be killed by a storm.

LYELL'S HYPOTHESES AGAIN

Charles Lyell published his *Principles of Geology* between 1830 and 1833.

ANDRÉE REXROTH

Mount Tamalpais

Mount Tamalpais is the tallest peak in Marin County, across the Golden Gate from San Francisco. Steep Ravine is a trail on the west side of Tamalpais, above Stinson Beach.

Kings River Canyon

Kings Canyon is the major canyon in the southern Sierra, one of
the deepest in North America. The road Rexroth mentions was
built in the early 1930s.

Henry King's seventeenth-century poem "The Exequy" (Latin
for funeral rites) is King's most famous poem.

Yuan Chen is a Chinese poet of the Tang dynasty (ninth century).

Frieda Lawrence moved back to New Mexico after D. H.
Lawrence's death.

BEYOND THE MOUNTAINS

Beyond the Mountains is a book of four one-act plays by Rexroth,
published by New Directions in 1951. All four of the plays are
concerned with the Bactrian-Greek civilization in the mountains
of Central Asia. An excellent essay about this book, written by
George Woodcock, appeared in *The Ark 14*, a 1980 festschrift called
"For Rexroth."

Included here are small excerpts from two of the plays, describ-
ing winter and mountain weather.

Final passage of THE DRAGON AND THE UNICORN

The Dragon and the Unicorn is a book-length poem, published by
New Directions in 1952. The method throughout alternates pas-
sages of philosophical speculation with a narration of Rexroth's
trip around the world in 1948, which came about as the result of
receiving a Guggenheim fellowship (See his letter thanking James
Laughlin for help with the Guggenheim on p. 178).

The last section of the book, included here, describes a trip
in the southern Sierra using so many places names that it is easy to
trace on a map (see pp. xx–xxi). It was one of Rexroth's usual trips
with horse and burro, starting at the west end of the High Sierra
Trail in Sequoia National Park. The High Sierra trail was built by

the CCC, and traverses the Sierra from Crescent Meadows in the west to Whitney Portal in the east.

Where the High Sierra trail merges with the Muir trail, Rexroth continued east off trail, up Wallace Creek (named after William Wallace of the copper mine in Deadman Canyon (see note for *Toward an Organic Philosophy*). The pack animals could not have gone higher than Wallace Lake; from there Rexroth continued up to Tulainyo Lake, which fills a dip on the crest of the range; at 12,800 feet, it is sometimes called the highest lake in North America. Only a hundred feet above it one stands on the crest, and therefore can see east over the Owens Valley to the Inyo Range, as Rexroth notes.

A LIVING PEARL

Mary Delia Andrée Rexroth was born to Kenneth and Marthe Larsen Rexroth in 1950, so this poem comes from 1951.

"The Okanogan and Horse Heaven country," and all the place names in the following lines, are in the North Cascades of Washington state.

There are two Mono Passes in the Sierra Nevada, one between Dana Meadows and Bloody Canyon in Yosemite, the other between Rock Creek and Mono Creek, farther to the south. Rexroth mentions crossing the northern Mono Pass with Andrée in his autobiographical novel. It was briefly a mining region, so the presence of an old miner's cabin indicates that here too he is referring to the northern Mono Pass.

THE LIGHTS IN THE SKY ARE STARS

See the essay by Carter Scholz on p. 184 for an explication of Rexroth's star references in this poem and others.

TIME IS THE MERCY OF ETERNITY
Black Rock Pass, 11,680 feet, is on the trail between Big Arroyo and
the Timber Gap (see map pp. xx–xxi). Rexroth probably rented
pack animals at Mineral King and headed north over the Timber
Gap to Black Rock Pass, but he also could have begun at Crescent
Meadows, gone east on the High Sierra Trail, then turned south
at Big Arroyo.

MARY AND THE SEASONS
All the sections of this poem reference plants and animals of the
Coast Range, except for the last one, "Another Twilight," which is
set in the Sierra somewhere, with a view west into the Great Central
Valley. See the Carter Scholz essay for the star references, (p. 184).

HOMER IN BASIC
In June 1957 Rexroth spent two weeks with his daughters Mary
and Katharine in the Giant Forest campground in Sequoia National
Park; this poem is from that stay.

FISH PEDDLER AND COBBLER
The Gros Ventre wilderness is in western Wyoming, just east of
Jackson. This poem is from August 1957, when Rexroth and his
daughters visited James and Ann Laughlin at their Snake River
Ranch, in Wilson, Wyoming.
    Rexroth refers here to his earlier mountain poem about Sacco
and Vanzetti, "Climbing Milestone Mountain, August 22,1937."

FROM AIR AND ANGELS
Maroon Bells is a peak and region in the Colorado Rockies.

From ONE HUNDRED POEMS FROM THE CHINESE (1956)
and ONE HUNDRED MORE POEMS FROM THE
CHINESE (1970)

Rexroth published two popular collections of translations from
Chinese poets, as well as two collections from Japanese poetry. In-
cluded are many different kinds of landscape poems. I have selected
a few here that are, to one degree or another, mountain poems.

> Tu Fu (713–770): One of the greatest Chinese poets, Sung
> dynasty.
>
> Ch'u Ch'uang I (early eighth century): A close friend of the
> poet Wang Wei.
>
> Wang Wei (701–761): The great mountain poet of the Tang
> dynasty.
>
> Liu Ch'ang Ch'ing (709–785): Poet of the Middle Tang Dy-
> nasty, with eleven poems in the popular anthology *Three
> Hundred Tang Poems.*
>
> Han Yu (768–824): Tang dynasty poet, one of the first Neo-
> Confucians.
>
> Li Shang Yin (813–859): Tang dynasty poet; Rexroth in his
> notes says, "Today Li Shang Yin is considered the greatest
> Tang poet after Po Chü-i."
>
> Wen T'ing Yen (ninth century): A friend of Li Shang Yin.

A SONG AT THE WINEPRESSES

Rexroth met Gary Snyder in the fall of 1953, and Rexroth in-
troduced Snyder to several local poets. In 1967 Rexroth and his
wife Carol visited Snyder and his wife Masa in Japan, and in 1969,
Snyder and Masa visited Rexroth and Carol at their home in Santa
Barbara. This poem seems to recall both visits. Between them,
these two poets have written much of the best poetry about the
Sierra Nevada.

Richard of St. Victor was born in Scotland, lived in Paris, and
was prior of the Augustinian Abbey of St. Victor from 1162 to 1173.
He was a prominent mystic and influential theological writer.

YOUR BIRTHDAY IN THE CALIFORNIA MOUNTAINS
The fifth and last in the sequence of memorial poems for Andrée
Rexroth, written in the early 1970s.

KENNETH REXROTH'S SIERRA PROSE

AN AUTOBIOGRAPHICAL NOVEL
The first edition of Rexroth's *An Autobiographical Novel* was pub-
lished in 1966. It ended at Chapter 10, shortly after Rexroth and his
first wife Andrée arrived in San Francisco and decided to live there,
in 1927. An expanded edition, published in 1991, added many chap-
ters and took Rexroth's story into the late 1940s. These chapters
naturally have more Sierra descriptions, as he was going up there
often during those years.

Rexroth always said the autobiographical novel was an accurate
account of his life, and was only titled "a novel" because the lawyers
at New Directions worried about the possibility of lawsuits from
people portrayed in it (see Laughlin's account in the passage from
Byways, p. 182). Others since have cast aspersions on its reliability,
without ever giving examples of lies or even distortions. So it has
been accused both of being *too* accurate and too full of stretchers.
Whatever the case may be, there is no reason to doubt anything
Rexroth had to say about his mountain experiences. Carter Scholz's
essay on Rexroth's star references (see p. 184) should make readers
think again about the veracity of Rexroth's memoirs. It will be

interesting to see if the new biography of Rexroth by Rachelle Lerner will address this topic.

Rexroth composed the book by dictating his account and then revising transcriptions of the recordings.

Chapter 39: Climbing Mt. Lyell would have taken them far up Lyell Canyon and away from shelter. Going over Mono Pass (north), it is likely they climbed Mt. Gibbs, not Mt. Gabb, which is near the other Mono Pass, far to the south. In this paragraph, Rexroth combines foot travel with automobile or bus travel; Lee Vining and Bridgeport are on Highway 395 in the Owens Valley, and with no good road over Tioga Pass in Yosemite, they apparently returned to San Francisco by going south of the Sierra and back up the Central Valley (see map, pp. xx–xxi).

Leo Eloesser (1881–1976) was, as Rexroth says, a leader in developing thoracic surgical techniques, and he gave his medical services to political prisoners and to the Republican forces in the Spanish Civil War.

Donner Lake and Castle Peak are near the crest of the Sierra Nevada, just to the north of Lake Tahoe.

Pacific Gas and Electric (PG&E) supplies electrical power to much of northern California, and built a vast network of hydro-electric dams and service roads in the Sierra in the early twentieth century.

Hume Lake is a reservoir on Tenmile Creek, a tributary of the Kings River, elevation 5,200 feet.

Boyden Cave is now located in Giant Sequoia National Monument, on Highway 180, and is open for tours April to November.

Chapter 52: Camp Singing Trail was run by Louis and Emma Blumenthal through the 1930s. A film about the camp was made in 1936 by the Blumenthals and is available online at: http://www.archive.org/details/cbm_00002.

Desolation Lake is a large lake in the Humphreys Basin, just west of Mount Humphreys (13,992 ft.). The summit past "Married Men's Point" is rated Class 5.4; the easiest route on the west side is rated Class 4, but is mostly Class 2, and is the likely route for the Rexroths.

Kings River Packing moves citrus from groves in the foothills to Visalia and Fresno. It is still in business but no longer uses burros.

Stewart Edward White (1871–1946) was an American writer who focused on the American West and the people living there. His book *The Pass* (1906) is an entertaining account of the discovery of Elizabeth Pass across the Kings-Kern Divide (Silliman Crest). The public campsite next to the Roaring River ranger station is still called The Stewart Edward White Camp.

The Sawtooth Ridge extends from Matterhorn Peak to Blacksmith Peak, on the northern border of Yosemite Park. A central section of this ridge is now called The Sawteeth, which is no doubt what Rexroth was referring to as "The Three Teeth." A traverse of the ridge involves a great deal of exposed Class 5 climbing.

In 1934, Maurice Wilson ("the insane Englishman") died on the north side of Everest during a solo attempt.

Chapter 53: Golden Trout Creek enters the Kern River twelve miles to the south of Whitney; the spot is far from any trailhead. The likely route for Rexroth and Marie was from Mineral King, over Florence and then Coyote Pass (see map, pp. xvi–xvii).

Chapter 60: The sheepherder's cabin that Rexroth used as a retreat for many years was located in one of the ravines on the south side of Devil's Gulch in Samuel P. Taylor State Park. The cabin fell apart in the 1950s. (See Rexroth's *Examiner* column, June 30, 1963).

The Phoenix and the Tortoise was published by New Directions in 1944. *The Signature of All Things* was published by New Directions in 1950.

The Libertarian Circle was an anarchist and literary club organized by Rexroth in 1945. The price of admission to meetings was a bottle of red wine. Participants included the poets William Everson, Robert Duncan, Jack Spicer, Muriel Rukeyser, and Thomas Parkinson. The club's readings spanned the history of anarchist thought, the goal being to "refound the radical movement after its destruction by the Bolsheviks and to rethink all the basic principles and subjects, searching criticism of all the ideologists from Marx to Malatesta."

CAMPING IN THE WESTERN MOUNTAINS

Rexroth was involved in a number of WPA projects in the mid-1930s, including organzing the mural painting on the inside of Coit Tower in San Francisco. He wrote part of the WPA's *Guide to California* (see p. 145), and also a camping guide, but the latter was never published. In 2003 Ken Knabb put the complete text online at the website www.bopsecrets.org/rexroth/camping/index.htm

As Knabb says in his online preface, "only in the present text can we really see how thoroughly familiar he was with just about every aspect of natural history and wilderness living."

The book would have been useful as a guide, but it is also entertaining. Several of the chapters are taken up by a detailed description of camping with pack animals rather than backpacking, although Rexroth recommends bringing backpacks along, and is clearly familiar with them; his description of how to make a backpack is a marvel of clearly written instructions. Although the materials used to make the gear have changed, much of the equipment he lists is necessary still, and in many cases his sense of appropriate gear is surprisingly contemporary: he prefers a tarp to a tent, he is familiar with air mattresses, and he declares that it's best to use them with sleeping bags that have sslots or extra layers to fit into, a design feature that is rare today, but useful.

The clear advantage of using pack animals was being able to bring along enough food for three or four weeks, along with miscellaneous gear to make camp more comfortable. Rexroth's minimum

list of gear would have weighed only thirty pounds or so, even made
of the materials of his time, and including the backpack; his food
allotment he calculated at two pounds two ounces per person per
day, again not much more than what is standard now. Backpacks
have practical limits in weight and volume, and one seldom tries to
carry more than two weeks' supplies. Using pack animals made a
month-long trip practical, and this was the norm for the Sierra Club
trips that began in the 1890s and continued into the late 1960s, when
the impact of such trips came to be seen as excessive and they were
stopped. It's the mark of a less driven age that so many middle-class
citizens were able to get a month of time off at once, and the Sierra
Club trips were family trips as well.

By the end of the 1950s a younger postwar generation was tak-
ing advantage of lighter and more compact gear, some of which had
been developed during the Second World War, and backpacking
became more popular as opposed to using pack animals. Typical
trips became shorter, but backpacking was in many ways simpler
and allowed one to get places animals could not go. It is also true
that as the number of Americans who knew how to care for pack
animals diminished, the packing companies stopped renting out
animals to individuals. Backpacking was enough the fashion in the
1960s that you can see Rexroth becoming a little defensive about
his family pack trips with his daughters; in his column for the *San
Francisco Examiner* he writes, "Just a square type outing." But hardly
any backpackers went out for a month at a time, and few went out
with their young daughters, so there were things to be said for the
older method.

Another tradition that ended for the good of the mountains
was the nightly campfire at tree line or above. Rexroth clearly had a
fire almost every night he was up there; his expertise in firewood is
revealed by his long lists of types of wood, ranked according to how
well they burned, and also by heat, lack of smoke, and longevity

of burn. No one today knows the characteristics of various types of mountain wood as well as Rexroth did, because no one makes back country fires as often as he did.

Chaper 6: This mention of "burmas" and "llaros" is Rexroth's little joke.

Chapter 9: In 1864 during the Geological Survey Expedition led by William Brewer, Clarence King and Richard Cotter left the camp near Mount Brewer in an attempt to climb the highest mountain on the Sierra Crest, which they had named Mount Whitney. They crossed the Kings-Kern Divide near Thunder Mountain and climbed a mountain on the crest they named Mount Tyndall. From its summit they could see that Mount Whitney was six miles farther south, and they didn't have the supplies to reach it.

Chapter 11: Edward Whymper was part of the first ascent of the Matterhorn, in 1865, achieved after several years of attempts. Four of the first party of seven died in the descent when a rope broke. See Whymper's *Scrambles Amongst the Alps* (1871), a book Rexroth refers to elsewhere.

Sir John Franklin and Fridtjof Nansen were Arctic explorers; Horace Benedict de Saussure was one of the earliest climbing scientists of the Swiss Alps.

A "good ski route" of the sort that Rexroth recommends is the "Sierra Ski High Route," a cross-country ski route on the Silliman Crest, developed in the 1970s. Rexroth recommends this as a hiking cross-country route in Chapter 10.

THE WPA GUIDE TO CALIFORNIA

In 1935, The Federal Writers' Project began a WPA-funded project to write automobile guides to every state; the idea for the series came from the poet Marianne Moore. Work on the series lasted until 1942. The California volume came out first under the title *Guide to the Golden State* in 1939. The 1984 reprint, titled *The WPA*

Guide to California, includes a new introduction by Gwendolyn Wright. She writes, "Poet Kenneth Rexroth's descriptions of the national parks—their forests, lakes, and deserts—are some of the most beautifully written passages in the guide." But there is little competition from the other passages. It is clear that Rexroth took the WPA guidelines seriously, and wrote in a "restrained and dignified style" with few personal touches or observations. Only the stories he tells reveal his point of view.

Hale D. Tharp (1828–1912) was a pioneer resident of Three Rivers and Giant Forest, California.

Lafayette Bunnell (1824–1903) was an American physician who made the first non-indigenous discovery of Yosemite Valley in 1851. He later served in the Civil War and wrote a book, *Discovery of the Yosemite, and the Indian War of 1851* (1880).

REXROTH'S NEWSPAPER COLUMNS IN THE *SAN FRANCISCO EXAMINER* AND THE *SAN FRANCISCO BAY GUARDIAN*

Ken Knabb's website has posted a selection of Rexroth's newspaper columns for the *San Francisco Examiner* and the *San Francisco Bay Guardian*. Currently Knabb is posting all of Rexroth's columns on the fiftieth anniversary of their first appearance.

Rexroth began writing columns for the *San Francisco Examiner* in 1961, and wrote about one a week until 1967. He had the space to write about anything that interested him, and over the years he covered topics literary, political, and cultural. Taken together they form an impressive if piecemeal education in the humanities, although it is also true that as the *Examiner* was a Hearst paper, Rexroth was often politically out of context. Still, the columns surely played their part in the lived experience of Bay Area culture in the 1960s.

Note the references to "tipover point" and "carbon dioxide in the atmosphere," and the idea of a phase change in culture as well as nature ("water turns into steam very quickly"). It was not so much a matter of Rexroth being prescient as being *au courant*; these ideas were part of the environmental movement throughout its rise in the 1960s. "A deadly crisis," Rexroth termed the environmental situation; the problems were recognized as being serious and widespread.

August 14, 1960: Hashknife Hartley was a cowboy character in books and on the radio in the 1930s.

Ernest Haycock (1899–1950) wrote Westerns from the 1920s through the 1940s. His work was admired by Gertrude Stein and Ernest Hemingway.

July 12, 1961: The Yosemite Park and Curry Company was the private concessionaire for Yosemite National Park from 1925 to 1993.

July 8, 1962: The Emigrant Basin is part of the Emigrant Wilderness, immediately to the north of Yosemite National Park.

Walter Paepcke (1896–1960) was an American industrialist and philanthropist who founded The Aspen Institute and The Aspen Ski Institute in the early 1950s.

Michael Murphy (b. 1930) founded The Esalen Institute at Big Sur in 1962.

August 21, 1963: Gifford Pinchot (1865–1946) was the first Head of the U.S. Forest Service (1905) and later was governor of Pennsylvania. He advocated sustainable use of wilderness and formulated an early "conservation ethic," a term he coined.

August 23, 1964: "Alice over in Africa ..." This is possibly a reference to Alice Sheldon, who was taken as a girl on a trip to Africa by her parents. Her mother, the travel writer Mary Hastings Bradley, later wrote two books called *Alice In Jungleland* and *Alice in Elephantland*. Sheldon grew up to become a science-fiction writer who wrote under the pen name James Tiptree, Jr.

January 24, 1966: The Disney Corporation's proposal to build a massive ski resort at the Mineral King trailhead was fought by the Sierra Club, in lawsuits that resulted in the project being denied in 1972.

Note Rexroth's quick definition of what is now called greenwashing, some forty years before the invention of the term itself; also his focus on the problem of topsoil loss, still as unsolvable as ever.

September 11, 1966: "Tipover point,": This concept, now called "tipping point," was analyzed and popularized in the 1980s by chaos theory, but it was also elucidated in nonlinear dynamics by Carl Friedrich Gauss in the eighteenth century.

"Dymaxion": Rexroth once met Buckminster Fuller, who used the term "dymaxion" to describe the form of his geodesic domes and many other structures.

The comparison of forests and lakes to hormones seems to suggest a kind of Gaia theory.

December 1969: The Workmen's Circle is an organization devoted to community building, begun by Jewish immigrants in New York City in 1900.

Lawrence Halprin (1916–2009) was an influential landscape architect based in San Francisco.

May 1969: Here we have a brief global analysis that includes carbon dioxide buildup, the possibility of a mass extinction event, extraction versus sustainability, the carrying capacity of the planet, a new socio-economic system designed for ecological balance— not only written in 1969, but claiming that all this had been clear for twenty-five years! It makes an impressive finish to Rexroth's mountain prose.

David Brower was president of the Sierra Club and lifelong leader of the environmental movement. There is an effort being made to rename North Palisade "Brower Palisade," and California senators Diane Feinstein and Barbara Boxer have introduced a bill to that effect.

CORRESPONDENCE AND COMMENTARY

From KENNETH REXROTH AND JAMES LAUGHLIN:
SELECTED LETTERS (1991)

The correspondence between Kenneth Rexroth and James Laughlin
was edited by Lee Bartlett and published in 1991 by W. W. Norton.
It is a fascinating exchange, but frustrating for readers interested in
their Sierra trips together, as they very rarely discuss them. The cor-
respondence is mostly taken up with discussions of the business and
politics of literature and publishing. The way Rexroth continually
badgers and insults Laughlin shows that he is comfortable saying
anything to his old mountain friend, and is suggestive of a rough
campside humor. Laughlin is wonderfully skillful at deflecting these
frequent attacks, but his later published comments about Rexroth
are a little ambivalent and barbed, as if the frequent insults and his
own easygoing replies had eventually taken their toll on him (see
Laughlin's *Byways* for an example where he is "getting even" with
Rexroth). Rexroth lost many friends over the years who could not
abide his temper, but possibly the mountain trips with Laughlin
made them deeper friends; some of the letters in their exchange
make it clear they were very close. In the end, Laughlin paid for the
private nursing Rexroth needed after his last strokes.

From THE WAY IT WASN'T, *by* JAMES LAUGHLIN

Some of Laughlin's reminiscences are collected in this alphabetically
arranged book. Rexroth takes up most of the entries for the letter R.

Delmore Schwartz (1913-1966) was an American writer pub-
lished throughout his career by James Laughlin. The correspondence
between these two men has been published (*Delmore Schwartz and
James Laughlin: Selected Letters*, ed. Robert Phillips, W.W. Norton,
1993).

From BYWAYS, *by* JAMES LAUGHLIN

This book contains a long, unfinished autobiographical poem in a verse form Laughlin learned from Rexroth, as he says on the first page.